CENTENNIAL COMMEMORATIVE
ISSUE
1871

This Book and its companion
pure silver Coin-medal are issued
to commemorate the 100th Anniversary
of the White Mountain Apache Reservation

———————

September 5, 1971

And is limited to 15,000 copies
No

Fred Banashley Sr

Western Ways Photograph by Charles W. Herbert
WHITE MOUNTAIN APACHE MEDICINE MAN blessing a girl and her ritual sponsor at the end of the four-day initiation ceremony, using sacred plant pollen.

THE

APACHE

PEOPLE

by *Henry F. Dobyns*

PUBLISHED BY INDIAN TRIBAL SERIES / PHOENIX

A STATEMENT
FROM THE TRIBAL CHAIRMAN

THE WHITE MOUNTAIN APACHE TRIBE extends an invitation to you to visit the Fort Apache Indian Reservation in East Central Arizona.

A century has passed since this area was set aside for the benefit of the White Mountain Apache people. For the past forty-five years, efforts have been made by the tribe to maintain an ecological balance to preserve the primitive, scenic areas for the enjoyment of those to follow. The Apache people invite you to choose a favorite campsite beside the many streams and lakes where rainbow trout abound, that have been improved for your enjoyment. Camp tables, fireplaces and other facilities have been constructed to make your stay comfortable. Thank you for your interest in the White Mountain Apache people and we hope that you enjoy our book and story and may someday come to Apache land. "Hon-Dah" is our Apache word of welcome to our homeland.

Hon-Dah

Fred Banashley Sr

FRED BANASHLEY, SR.
Apache Tribal Chairman

WHITE MOUNTAIN APACHE CHIEF ALCHESAY as he appeared during the first decade of reservation life and Indian Scouting.

A PACHE!
That word struck terror in the hearts of generations of White frontiersmen in northern New Spain and the Southwestern United States. Apache Indians conducted one of the longest, most effective guerilla wars, resisting European conquest longer than any native people in the world. As a result, Spaniards, Mexicans and Anglo-Americans heaped epithets on them: murderous and miserable, brutal and blood-thirsty, impracticable but deceitful, cunning, cowardly, cruel, savage and treacherous. Such is the vocabulary of cultural difference and conflict.

The bellicosity and tactics of the Apaches stemmed more from geopolitical necessity than personal inclination or cultural conditioning. Throughout most of historic times, Apaches found themselves caught between mighty forces

1

of expanding European nations and Indian tribes at the edges of the world commercial market. The northward advance of Spanish New World imperialism ran head-on into Apachean peoples. For a brief time, Apacheans who stole Spanish horses enjoyed the superiority of mounted warriors over neighboring Indian foot troops. They expanded eastward and northward. Before many decades passed, French and British traders supplied enemy tribes with guns and munitions. Then Apaches suffered decisive defeats by better-armed tribes and fled southward to survive. For 150 years after 1725, Apaches struggled to survive between the hammer of Plains tribes mounted and armed with guns, and the anvil of a fortified Spanish frontier.

THE PEOPLE

Apache Indians speak dialects of a language linguists call Southern Athapascan. Other Indians in Canada and northern California speak northern Athapascan. Speakers of Southern Athapascan became known during historic times as Navajos and Apaches. All these groups refer to themselves as *Dine'*, a term best translated as "The People" or "Human Beings." White Mountain Apache people living on Fort Apache Reservation in eastcentral Arizona today are descended from five bands making up what Spaniards called Coyotero Apaches plus a scattering of individuals from other bands.

The bulk of the White Mountain Apaches consists of descendents of Eastern and Western White Mountain Bands and the Cibecue, Carrizo and Canyon Creek Bands. Ranging at the northern extreme of Western Apacheria after 1700, these bands lived immediately south of the Navajos. Genetically and culturally they were transitional between Navajos and other Western Apaches. White Mountain Apaches inherit clan membership from their mothers and must marry outside their own clan. Thus, a man usually moves to his wife's camp when he marries.

Economically, Navajos revolutionized their culture by adopting sheep as an economic base and absorbing Pueblo refugees from the 1680 Pueblo Revolt described in *The Hopi People*. Lipan, Mescalero and Chiricahua Apaches revolutionized their culture by raiding Spanish and Indian settlements for food, livestock and slaves. The ancestors of the White Mountain Apaches remained less extreme, relied more on hunting, food collecting and horticulture and remained intermediate in ritual. Spaniards lumped the five bands under the label *Coyoteros,* the term that provides the title for this volume.

ABORIGINAL ECONOMY

When Francisco Vazquez de Coronado explored the southern Plains in 1540, he saw some

Apachean people. Whether he encountered Coyoteros or not, his description almost certainly applied to most Apacheans of that era. They moved over vast plains hunting bison, assisted by large dogs harnessed to travois (burden-carriers with trailing ends tied in a point skidding over the earth). Using dogs as beasts of burden increased mobility, yet left a strict limit on tent size and quantity of food, water and tools they could transport. Apacheans at that time evidently practiced horticulture in favorable river valleys during the summer.

Southern Plains tribes carried on a lively trade with eastern Pueblo Indians in modern New Mexico. The plainsmen bartered dressed bison hides, buckskins and meat for agricultural products. Men traded, fought, hunted, made their own weapons and helped with heavy work. Women collected and processed plant foods, gardened, fashioned household utensils, cooked, cared for small children and erected tipis.

Mounted Warfare

Spaniards colonized the upper Río Grande Valley in 1598, bringing large numbers of livestock. Early in the next century, Apacheans began to acquire horses. Probably Apacheans trading in Pueblos simply stole them. The Apacheans soon emulated Spanish cavalry tactics. Mounted on horseback, protected by leather armor and shields and armed with

4

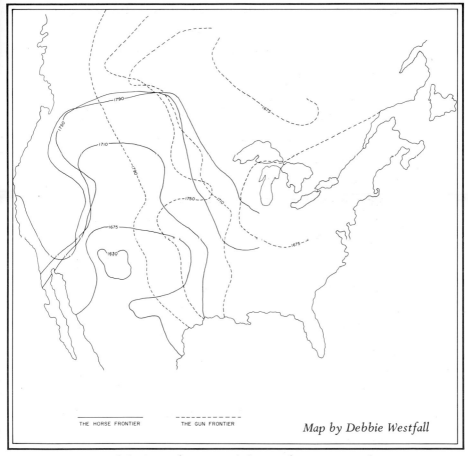

THE HORSE FRONTIER THE GUN FRONTIER *Map by Debbie Westfall*

MAP 1. Movement of the horse frontier and the gun frontier in North America.

Spanish-style lances as well as their own bows and arrows, Apacheans quickly won military superiority over neighboring tribes which did not yet possess mounts.

Before Apacheans acquired horses and employed cavalry battle tactics, superior manpower held the key to Indian military success. Warriors fought in half-moon shaped formations so that the force with the longer line could turn the flanks of the smaller group and rout it. Horses and lances enabled Apacheans to defeat native infantry regardless of numerical disparities. The "Horse Frontier" of 1675 shown on Map 1 can be interpreted as primarily an Apachean tertitorial frontier, suggesting the rapidity and scale of Apachean expansion beginning around 1650.

Those southern Athapascans who became known as Navajos already lived west of the Río Grande, at least in part, by the end of the first third of the 1600's. If the Coyotero and other Western Apaches remained east of the Río Grande early in that century, they had moved well west of it by the end. The 1680 Pueblo Revolt and its aftermath of extensive population movements carried Western Apache bands well beyond the Río Grande into territory that became their permanent habitat. That mountainous region eventually provided Western Apache bands with most names by which they are known to history.

The Spanish frontier in Coahuila, Chihuahua and Sonora lay far south of the New Mexican province temporarily destroyed by the Pueblo Revolt. On those frontiers north of the sedentery Conchos Indians and east of the Opatas, the Spaniards initially encountered several small Indian groups they termed Sumas, Janos, Jumanos and nomadic Mansos. Whether some or all of them spoke southern Athapascan cannot be determined from scant surviving evidence. At least seven Indian groups competed for meager resources in an unproductive desert country at the end of the 17th Century. Some, if not all, seem to have been newcomers, perhaps dislodged by Apachean expansion during the period of military supremacy of mounted warriors.

These northern Chihuahua Indians, especially the Sumas, rebelled against Spanish colonial rule in 1684. The Spaniards responded with punitive expeditions and a fort established at Janos in 1685 and another at Fronteras in 1690. First Sumas and then Janos led Indian resistance. By the early 1700's, however, Spaniards consistently referred to hostile Indians on the Sonora-Chihuahua frontier as "Apaches." Zuñi Pueblo evidently supplied frontier Spanish with this term synonymous with "enemy." During the twenty years after the Janos fort was founded,

7

Sumas, Jocomes, Janos and Mansos either moved elsewhere, were exterminated, or merged with Apachean bands.

Southwestward-moving Apacheans established hostile contact with Northern Piman Indians on the Spanish frontier in Sonora in 1697. Northern Piman Indians, inhabiting the San Pedro and Gila River Valleys in modern southern Arizona, constituted the native military barrier against which the southwestward wave of Apachean expansion broke. Spanish settlers north of the new forts retreated, however, leaving Apaches occupying a 250-mile wide territory south of Zuñi Pueblo to Janos that separated Spanish New Mexico from Sonora.

By the beginning of the 18th Century, Western Apache bands had already shifted from bison hunting to economic raiding combined with mountain game hunting and wild plant food gathering. Apache hunters employed stealth, decoys, surrounds and firedrives to kill deer, elk, antelope, javalina, mountain lions and small game such as hares, rabbits, porcupines and rats. They fashioned durable buckskin moccasins with upturned toes, buckskin breechclouts, and used stout oak, mulberry or locust wood bows and cane or hardwood arrows. Such few firearms as they possessed they had to seize from Spaniards by force, along with powder and balls, metal tools of all kinds, tipi canvas and shirts, drawers, vests and hats. Besides factory

Western Ways Photo by Charles W. Herbert

WHITE MOUNTAIN APACHE WOMAN brushing spines off ripe prickly pear (*Opuntia sp.*) cactus fruits she picks into her hand-made basket. She wears the woman's costume adopted when Army restrictions on movement ended hunting frequently enough to provide buckskins for clothing.

products they could obtain only forcibly, Western Apaches took anything else of utility they could during raids, especially livestock, hides, cereals and slaves. The Spaniards set them the example of slaving by seizing numerous Apache captives or purchasing them from frontier tribesmen.

Soon after 1700, French and British traders penetrating the North American continent carried the manufactured products of industrializing Europe to tribes on the Apachean borders. By 1720 to 1727, several tribes that Apacheans had pushed north or east acquired sufficient firearms and munitions to defeat the eastern Apacheans decisively. Apachean domination of the southern Plains was reversed. Tribes armed with guns ousted Apacheans from the Plains, especially after the Comanche and Caddo formed an alliance in 1740. From that time on, the Lipan, Mimbreño and Mescalero tribes became somewhat clearly identified in Spanish records as the only Apaches disputing portions of the southern Plains with the better-armed Comanches. They alternately harassed and sheltered behind Spanish border posts. The Plains Apache collapse exposed more westerly bands to raids by aggressive Plains tribes such as the Comanches. Those "Lords of the South Plains" set the eastern limit of Western Apache territory at the Pecos River. Probably in response, western Apache raiders after 1730

10

opened regular corridors between Spanish forts to strike ranches south of Arispe on the Sonora River, mines south of Cumpas on the Moctezuma and even the upper Yaqui River.

Northern Piman Indians rebelled against Spanish rule in 1751, expelling Spaniards from their territory in northern Sonora. The Spaniards defeated them in 1752 and established a new fort at Tubac on the Santa Cruz River, about 50 miles behind the Apache frontier. The Northern Pimans suffered serious depopulation from Old World diseases during the 18th Century. Consequently, their San Pedro River Valley population fell by 1762 below the minimum they felt necessary to maintain adequate defense and social organization. They abandoned the San Pedro and retreated to the Santa Cruz River Valley. Although they hunted, collected acorns and roasted agave in the mountains east of the Santa Cruz, their retreat opened the area to Western Apache hunting, mescal roasting, and travel south into Sonora. Former Piman haunts became Western Apache staging areas for raids.

By 1775, the Spaniards recognized a need to push their military frontier northward. The frontier Inspector General examined a site across the Santa Cruz River from the Indian mission at Tucson and ordered the Tubac garrison to move there. Colonial authorities expected this post to protect the flank of an overland route from

Sonora to Upper California. Actually, it drew attacks. Plains Indian pressure may have become especially heavy, motivating the Western Apaches to mount frequent large-scale raids to attempt to seize significant quantities of metal tools and guns and munitions. On the other hand, Western Apaches may have felt that they were strong enough to challenge directly Spanish military superiority. Whatever the reason, an estimated 350 Apaches approached Tucson in 1779, a force its garrison defeated in the field. Then a large Apachean force attacked Tucson on May Day, 1782. The behavior of the assault force indicated that its commander or commanders intended to seize the fort if possible. Surprising the under-manned post with its main gate open, the Apaches repeatedly tried to storm the entrance. The post commandant personally stood off Apache assaults at the gate, assisted by only a few troopers. The garrison lieutenant, caught in his house outside the stockade, brought the attackers under murderous cross-fire from his parapet, assisted by a valient Indian servant. The Spaniards held by a narrow margin. This assault by an estimated 600 Apaches and similar attempts on other posts marked a high water mark in Western Apache audacity and organization. In 1784, Gila Apaches reportedly enlisted Navajo aid in attempts to storm both Tucson and Janos.

During the century between 1684 and 1785,

then, the Western Apaches occupied at least a partially new habitat and modified their cultural patterns to capitalize upon its varied resources. They continued living in skin-covered dwellings up to the end of the 18th Century, using cowhide or horsehide when they could not obtain bison skins. This appeared to be a persistance of Plains behavior in the Southwestern environment. Great variations in altitude gave Western Apaches a broad choice of edible plants, and they made use of over 100 different species, with tree seeds (pinyon nuts, juniper berries, acorns and mesquite pods) and agave hearts most important. The seasonal movement of Western Apaches depended upon the ripening of plant foods at different elevations in varied ecological niches more than upon raiding. Spring sent women searching for budding agave plants to cut, trim, pit-roast, feast on and sun-dry. Gardening families cleared fields, repaired ditches and planted in May. Leaving some oldsters to watch the growing crops, they moved down to the desert mountains in July to harvest giant cactus fruit. Toward the end of that month, they harvested seed-bearing annuals and picked berries. Then they gathered acorns. Late August and September took people to the desert again for mesquite pods, cactus and yucca fruits. Garden produce was ready for harvesting in late September or October, followed by pinyon nuts and juniper berries. November to April brought

13

time free from the wild food quest to hunt, visit, rest and raid.

The 1684 and 1751 Indian revolts on the Chihuahuan and Sonoran frontiers of New Spain opened areas to Western Apaches. Spanish forts at Janos, Tucson and Tubac contained the Apache advance. The frontier line remained a paper curtain Apache raiders punctured at will, gradually forcing Spanish settlers and Opata Indians southward in Sonora.

One military advantage Western Apaches enjoyed over Spaniards was a long-range communication system. Many a joke about Indian smoke-signals has been published, but smoke messages constituted no joke to Spaniards. Each Apache carried fire-making materials, and all understood a standard set of meanings of smoke made in a variety of topographical situations, sizes and durations. Exposing and covering fires sent the same messages at night. The Spanish army lacked any comparable mobile, long-distance communication system. So did the U. S. Army until it adopted the heliograph to run down the last few score of hostile Apaches.

While they occupied new territory, the Western Apaches nonetheless depended on sedentary settlements for their economic well-being. They lived in good part on horses and cattle they drove off, from grain and other produce of industrious Indian horticulturalists. Raiding constituted the main business activity of

Western Apaches. Since it was in the Apache interest to maintain a dependable supply of food and mounts, they did not strive to kill those whom they raided. Only when very large, multi-band Apachean forces achieved a measure of surprise did they attack Spanish forts, evidently hoping to obtain numbers of firearms and stores of powder and balls for long-range combat. Native bows and arrows, stone-headed war clubs and cowhide shields and wooden lances modeled on Spanish patterns more than adequately armed Western Apaches for close combat.

Basically, the White Mountain Apaches supplemented their hunting, gathering and horticulture with proceeds of raiding along corridors well known to them far south into Sonora. In effect, all Western Apaches adjusted to the realities of world power during the 1684-1785 century by occupying that Southwestern territorial niche not interdicted to them by superior Indian or Spanish power, and exploiting a supplemental range far to the south through economic raiding. Although Western Apache bands lived and generally raided separately, a few Apache assault forces reached so large a scale as to evidence multiple band leadership. Probably the near uniformity of Apache cultural response to the opportunities and limitations of the colonial frontier environment also reflected band chief discussions and

15

consensus, if not formal government of larger social units.

SPANISH PACIFICATION, 1786-1821

A general process of institutional reform under the Bourbon Kings of Spain, coupled with Apachean assaults on frontier military posts early in the 1780's produced a basic change in colonial policy toward Apacheans. In 1786, the new Viceroy of New Spain ordered that Apacheans, with whom peace treaties had not been allowed, would be encouraged to sue for peace. This meant that powerful Spanish cavalry columns would comb Apachería for settlements to attack so as to persuade Apaches that their survival depended upon ending hostilities. Those who sued for peace were to settle beside frontier military posts, where they would be fed Spanish rations, including spirituous liquors, and allowed to trade while encouraged to learn Spanish cultural patterns. The King made the orders royal policy in 1787.

During the latter years of that decade, tremendously improved Spanish frontier garrisons carried out a series of hard-hitting and effective search-and-destroy missions into Western and southern Apachería. Spaniards and their Northern Piman and Opata Indian allies found and destroyed many an Apache *ranchería*. They slew large numbers of Apaches, captured others.

The able Spanish Governor of New Mexico,

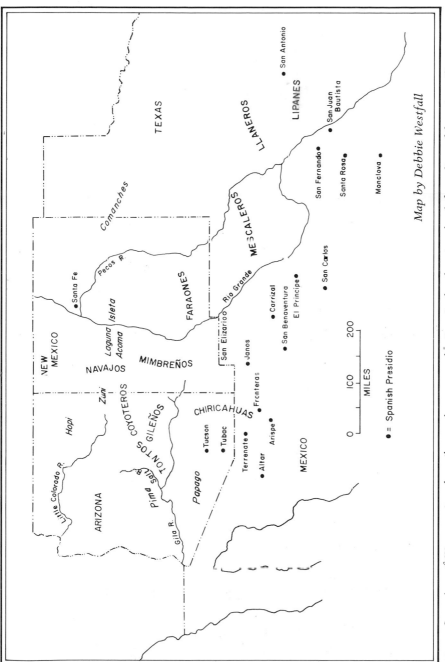

MAP 2. Location of Western Apache tribes as known to the Spaniards, showing the defense line of frontier military posts.

Map by Debbie Westfall

Colonel Juan Bautista de Anza, during this period successfully pursued a policy of separating Navajos from Western Apaches. Concluding an alliance with Comanches, Anza was able to bring tremendous pressure upon the Navajos by threatening to unleash Comanches and Utes on them if they did not cooperate with the Spaniards against Western Apaches. Anza's prohibition against Navajo trade with Pueblos and Spaniards generated a Navajo 1785 campaign against White Mountain Apaches, in this case called Gileños. Thus, Anza accelerated cultural differentiation between the shepherd Navajos and raiding bands of Western Apaches. Comanche allies as well as Pueblo auxiliaries accompanied a Spanish expedition into the Apachería southwest of the Hopi villages in September of 1787, into either Tonto or Cibecue Band Apache country.

Harried by strong Spanish strikes deep into Apachería, many bands sued for peace and agreed to live in what amounted to Indian reservations under military control. Chiricahua Apaches congregated at the Spanish fort of Bacoachi, Sonora, beginning in September, 1786. In 1787, Mescaleros began settling at El Paso and Mimbreños at San Buenaventura and in 1790 at Janos. Members of at least the Arivaipa and Pinal Bands settled at Tucson in 1793 and later. Significantly, Mexican oral tradition at Tucson identified the Apaches who helped to erect the first mission church there as Coyoteros. That tradition suggests that the Coyoteros were more receptive toward European cultural influences than other Western Apaches, and that they were also more concerned over their relationship to the supernatural.

By 1795, Spanish pacification progressed to the point that a Spanish column could march from Tucson to Zuñi and back across the Apachería. As far as available records show, that was only the second successful Spanish march across Apachería since the mid-1600's. Its commander considered Zuñi to be endangered by Coyoteros south of the Pueblo in the Pinal Mountains.

The "Tamed Apaches" learned to eat Spanish foods, so the tortilla became a staple food. They learned to wear some Spanish-style clothing, to gamble with Spanish playing cards, to drink distilled alcoholic beverages and to brew *tulapai* of sprouted maize kernels. Certainly those Apache bands subsisting on Spanish rations they eked out with game learned many cultural lessons living cheek by jowl with Spanish soldiery — including crop irrigation techniques. The era of peaceful symbiotic relations between Spaniards and Peaceful Apaches endured as long as the Spanish Empire.

MEXICAN-APACHE WARFARE, 1830-1853

Not long after Mexico won political indepen-

19

dence from Spain, new factors turned Apaches to the warpath. For a decade following independence, the new Mexican government continued colonial Apache policy. Soon after independence, however, major military forces and economic resources poured down the drain of continual struggles for political supremacy in central Mexico. Consequently, rations destined for Apaches living peacefully at frontier posts diminished and arrived sporadically if at all. Thus most Apaches had little inducement to remain at the forts, and many for hunting, gathering and raiding.

At about the same time, aggressive United States citizens engaged in the fur trade and general commerce began to arrive in Coyotero territory with firearms and munitions to trade. At least some gun-runners appear consciously to have aimed to foster the Manifest Destiny of the United States by weakening Mexican border defenses. This they accomplished by providing Apaches with efficient firearms.

By 1830, therefore, at least some Western Apache bands had turned to economic raiding of Mexican and Northern Piman and Opata Indian settlements. Western Apaches resumed intensive raiding in 1831, ending forty to forty-five years of peaceful reservation life. Mexican authorities estimated they killed 5,000 persons and caused 4,000 to move from raided areas by 1835. Bands that had lived at Spanish-Mexican forts enjoyed

20

tremendous advantages when they turned to raiding. They shared a great deal of Mexican knowledge and often owned good firearms. They understood Mexican military tactics, and knew intimately the geography of Mexican frontier defense and settlement. Armed with weapons manufactured in the U. S., Apaches could accurately claim that the northern Mexicans became their herders. As a matter of fact, Western Apache bands waxed rather wealthy in terms of horses and cattle stolen from Mexicans.

Beyond purely economic benefits of raiding peasants for livestock and agricultural produce, Apache warriors enjoyed the sexual delights of nubile female captives. The Western bands captured and kept physically pleasing Mexican girls and women, Northern Piman, Opata and Yaqui Indian women. Thus, the return to warfare eventually markedly altered the genetic makeup of Western Apaches. Half-Apache offspring of captive women grew up as Apaches, along with captive children, thus introducing a physical variation into the population that had not previously existed. Incorporation of adult women into the Apache population also undoubtedly brought cultural influences to housekeeping, domestic arts such as basket making, desert plant use, etc.

During this period of wartime prosperity, Western Apache bands lived not only on captured foodstuffs, but also from hunting still-abundant game in the mountains, and from collecting wild foods and growing crops. If Western Apaches had not known how to irrigate maize, squash and beans prior to their peaceful residence beside Spanish-Mexican irrigators, they certainly learned how to build diversion dams and dig irrigation ditches during their semi-captivity. One ditch irrigated five to fifteen farms, and ditch bosses supervised dam and ditch repairs and water distribution. Almost certainly Western Apaches borrowed this form of social organization from peasant irrigators between 1790 and 1830. At least as early as 1830 a Mexican expedition commander reported finding impressive irrigation works in use by what may have been the San Carlos or a Coyotero band.

Confronted with a shortage of federal government subsidies to maintain Peaceful Apaches at peace, Sonoran and Chihuahuan state officials reverted to the Apache extermination policy that colonial Spain abandoned as unsuccessful. Even though the federal government could or would not transmit funds for Apache rations, state treasuries found coins and currency to offer a hundred dollar bounty on each Apache scalp. The genocidal policy of the States succeeded no better than it had in colonial times. In fact, the Apaches forced Mexican abandonment of Tubac briefly, seized control of Fronteras, raided the state capital city, and struck deep into Papago Indian country, and to the Gulf of California and south to the tropic fruit-growing valleys. State and federal Mexican forces appeared powerless to curb Apache incursions. The main Coyotero plunder trail passed near Fronteras en route from the trans-Gila homeland into central Sonora.

What the extermination policy did accomplish was to further isolate Western Apaches, and awaken their hatred of Anglo-American scalp hunters. The Apaches isolated themselves by classifying all sedentary Indians south of them as sources of booty. Although Western Apaches traded with Pueblo Indians northeast of them, they created a tangible social barrier of enmity between themselves and other Indians, save for cultural transfers stemming from slavery. Part of the barrier in the 19th Century consisted of Apache political fragmentation. Political authority of a given leader usually extended no farther than his immediate band. Thus, forty to fifty raid organizers decided peace, war, strategy and tactics. Mexican and U. S. authorities consistently overestimated the number of Apaches following chiefs they met, so blamed them for perfidy when all Western Apaches failed to observe terms of an agreement with one or two leaders.

Yet Apaches faced a similar dilemma. Towns in Chihuahua bought booty taken in Sonora. New Mexican towns purchased spoils seized in

Chihuahua, etc. While most of the peaceful Apaches broke with the Mexicans early in the 1830's, some remained faithful to their army associates. Groups of *Apaches Mansos* continued to live at Tucson, Janos, San Buenaventura, Galeana, Tubac and other settlements throughout the Mexican period. They campaigned as scouts with Mexican forces, opposing their hostile relatives, and also fought independently, if not slaughtered by scalp hunters. Those at Tubac and Tucson served U. S. forces as scouts, and disappeared into the general population after the United States annexed the area.

UNITED STATES SOVEREIGNTY, 1848-1971

When the United States went to war with Mexico in 1846, the Western Apaches welcomed U. S. troops as allies against a common enemy. U. S. forces benefited from good will built up by Anglo-American gun-runners. The Coyoteros consistently maintained friendliness toward U. S. citizens despite two decades of inconsistent treatment, treachery and abuse. Other Western Apaches regarded as ridiculous the Anglo-American notion that U. S. conquest of Mexico bestowed on the U. S. ownership of Apache lands that Mexico had not controlled. Western Apaches and Sonorans continued to mount raid and counter-raid, while many Apaches felt that their peace with Anglo-Americans legitimized their war with the Mexican enemy.

24

In 1853, the United States added the Gadsden Purchase area south of the Gila River to the present international boundary between Arizona and Sonora. That made pacification of the Western Apaches very distinctly a U. S. responsibility and military problem, since all of these Indians save for the southern band of Chiricahuas then resided within the United States. Not until the middle of the decade, however, was the U. S. able to take physical possession of the purchase area by stationing regular army troops there. By that time many Western Apaches had stolen or purchased U. S.-made guns that emigrants traded for food en route west.

Throughout the long history of conflict between the southern bands of Western Apaches with Anglo-Americans, the relatively peaceful behavior of northern bands stands out. The pacifism of the White Mountain Apaches began to come to the attention of U. S. authorities at least by the early 1850's. In 1852, a group of Apaches who were probably Coyoteros from the White Mountains made a peace agreement at Acoma Pueblo. In 1853, Dr. Michael Steck began acting as resident agent to the Western Apache bands known to treaty-makers as Gila Apaches. With his encouragement, the Gileños raised good crops the first year they farmed on a reservation, and produced a significant surplus the second year. The Gileño settlements attracted White Mountain Band visitors, and Agent

25

Steck unofficially cultivated their friendship. He applauded their "reliableness" and horticultural productivity. He estimated 2,500 Coyoteros included 600 warriors. Steck also treated with Coyoteros and Pinal Apaches in late 1859 at Pueblo Viejo, Arizona, encountering again an advanced horticultural technology among the former. Meanwhile, Cibecue and Canyon Creek Band Apaches shared maize, copper and calico that the Anglo-Americans distributed about 1859 at Cañada del Oro near Tucson. Western Apaches at that time appeared willing to grant Anglo-Americans passage through their territory — for a fee — although not to permit unrestricted settlement nor to stop raiding into Mexico. Steck proved that some, at least, of the northern bands sincerely desired a peaceful way of life based upon intensive agriculture. This relative pacifism continued even after the Anglo-American-hating Chief Mangas Coloradas married one of his half-Mexican daughters to a Coyotero war chief as he forged widespread personal ties.

Events on the eastern seaboard postponed pacific interethnic relations between Apaches and Anglo-Americans. Just as Steck and a few others proved that peaceful relations between Western Apaches and Anglo-Americans were possible, civil war began in the East. The great scale of conflict beginning in 1861 led to prompt withdrawal of regular army units from

26

the western territories to the main theaters of war. Before they left, however, a lieutenant fresh from the United States Military Academy curriculum, totally deficient in social science instruction, murdered several Apache hostages and set off bitter hostilities.

Within a few months, California Volunteers re-garrisoned the posts in New Mexico Territory (which then included Arizona). Cochise joined forces with Mangas Coloradas to try to block a volunteer column at Apache Pass in 1862. Only then did even the Chiricahuas mobilize 200 to 300 warriors on something resembling the scale of Apachean fort assault forces collected in the 1780's.

Having secured the Río Grande Valley for the Union, General James H. Carleton launched campaigns to pacify key hostile Indians. In order to relieve Indian military pressure on the Río Grande Valley population, Carleton initiated a determined assault upon the Navajos. Led by Colonel "Kit" Carson, U. S. forces decisively defeated the Navajos, gathered most of them up to be interned at Fort Sumner in eastern New Mexico. That U. S. military achievement basically altered the strategic position of White Mountain Apaches. In effect, earlier exploration of the Beale Wagon Road from Zuñi Pueblo to the Colorado River in 1858 drove an opening wedge between Navajos and White Mountain Apaches. Carson's defeat of the Navajos and

27

their removal to Fort Sumner turned the northern flank of Apachería, leaving completely open to Anglo-American attack what had historically been the most secure border of Western Apache country. It brought U. S. forces north of the White Mountain Apaches, and denied them an historic refuge area to the north, as well as any future military alliances with the soundly defeated and permanently pacified Navajos. The Coyoteros continued, nonetheless, to trade with the Zuñi and Hopi Pueblos.

Even while civil conflict raged to the East, Carleton extended a ring of U. S. forts around White Mountain Apache territory. Carleton responded to the Chiricahua attempt to block Apache Pass by re-inforcing Fort Webster in southwestern New Mexico, re-establishing Fort Breckenridge (later re-named Camp Grant) at the confluence of Arivaipa Creek with the San Pedro River on 18 May 1862, and founding Fort Bowie in Chiricahua territory on 28 June 1862, as well as re-garrisoning Tucson and Tubac. When prospectors discovered gold near Prescott in 1863, the Army promptly established a post on the western periphery of Western Apache country within Yavapai territory, originally as Camp Clark at Del Río Springs in Chino Valley on 21 December. It was renamed Fort Whipple when removed to Granite Creek on 18 May 1864. Soon the Army added Fort Goodwin in Pinal Band territory on the Gila River. Chief

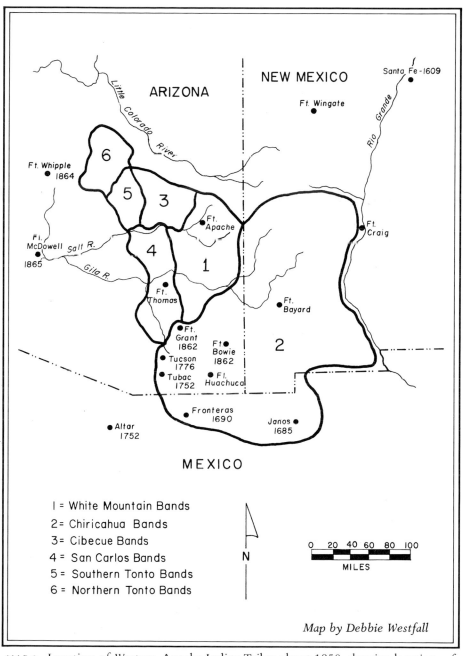

NEW MEXICO

ARIZONA

Santa Fe-1609

Ft. Wingate

Little Colorado River

Rio Grande

Ft. Whipple
1864

6

5

3

Ft.
Apache

Ft.
Craig

Ft.
McDowell
1865

Salt R.

Gila R.

4

1

Ft.
Thomas

Ft.
Grant
1862

Ft.
Bayard

Ft.
Bowie
1862

2

Tucson
1776

Tubac
1752

Ft.
Huachuca

Fronteras
1690

Janos
1685

Altar
1752

MEXICO

1 = White Mountain Bands
2 = Chiricahua Bands
3 = Cibecue Bands
4 = San Carlos Bands
5 = Southern Tonto Bands
6 = Northern Tonto Bands

N

0   20 40 60 80 100

MILES

Map by Debbie Westfall

MAP 3. Location of Western Apache Indian Tribes about 1850, showing locations of principal United States military posts involved in their pacification.

Diablo represented the White Mountain Apaches at a council with Army officers there making peace.

On September 7, 1865, five California Volunteer companies established Fort McDowell on the west bank of the Verde River seven miles above its mouth, at the Southern edge of Yavapai and Tonto Apache Band range, to protect the Gila River Pima and Maricopa and the Papago Indians. In mid-1866, California Volunteers started Camp Wallen on Babocomeri Creek. For the first time, U. S. Army garrisons stretched across Western Apache territory.

Once the federal union had been preserved, professional soldiers who remained in the army turned to fighting Indians. Western Apaches became a primary target for forceful pacification with extermination the alternative, on grounds they had taken advantage of the weakening of U. S. garrisons. Regular army detachments replaced volunteer units and founded additional strong points. Regulars set up Camp Crittenden on Sonoita Creek on 10 August 1867, and others established Camp Reno east of the Mazatzal Mountains on 11 October 1867. While no officer equalled Carson's swift Navajo pacification, the Indian-fighting Army did bring superior weapons and logistical support to bear to wear down the Western Apaches.

Anglo-American settlers in the new Arizona Territory clamored for an Apache extermination policy. From time to time they did their best to implement it with assistance from Pimas, Papagos, Maricopas, and Mexican-Americans who chose to remain in the annexed area. They lacked sufficient manpower to succeed, however, and differences in personal views of federal officers between 1865 and 1871 meant in effect that the national government followed no consistent policy at all. White Mountain Apaches remember suffering from the extermination policy when a number of them died from eating dried meat distributed at an encampment at Goodwin Springs.

Fort Apache

The early years of U. S. sovereignty over Apachería produced a whole series of gradations in intensity and type of contact between Apaches and Anglo-Americans. Although involved in peace negotiations in the 1850's and with their northern flank turned since 1863, the Coyoteros remained perhaps least exposed to Anglo-Americans prior to 1869. Prospectors had not discovered valuable minerals in their territory and settlers had not yet invaded their lands. They devoted themselves to hunting, food collecting and crop cultivation without becoming involved in the hostilities characterizing southern Arizona Territory. They did still raid into Mexico for livestock, arms and metals.

Then 1869 proved a turning point in Coyo-

31

tero history. At the national policy making level, concern over Indian affairs throughout the country led President U. S. Grant to appoint a Board of Indian Commissioners to establish a new humane federal Indian policy. At the local level, Colonel John Green marched into White Mountain Apache country in July, 1869, in command of 130 men. Green's orders called for him to seek a suitable area in which to establish an Indian reservation, and also to locate a good site for yet another military post. Learning that Apaches north of his route were growing large quantities of maize, Green sent a captain with sixty men on an extermination mission. The Apaches so impressed Captain John Barry with their desire for peace, however, that he ignored those orders, and was later exonerated of blame for doing so. The expedition commander reported that the Coyoteros could form a nucleus for civilizing all Apaches if protected by a reservation and military post. Descendants of Chief Diablo claimed that White Mountain chief granted permission to U. S. authorities to build the road and fort, indicating the White Mountain Apache desire for peace.

When General George Stoneman assumed command of the new Military Department of Arizona, he assigned Col. Green to execute the plan for permanent pacification of the Coyoteros. Green constructed a road into the center of the region set apart as a reserve, establishing a

INDIAN SCOUTS DRIVING FREIGHT WAGONS on the road to Fort Apache. Freighting supplies over Colonel John Green's wagon road became a principal duty of White Mountain Apache Indian Scouts. This 20th Century photograph indicates that the road never really improved much.

post at its terminus on 16 May 1870. First labeled Camp Ord, that post later became known as Camp Mogollon, Camp Thomas and Fort Apache. Over 1,000 Apaches appeared on 1 July to be counted and issued beef for the first time. By mid-September a post trader was brewing lager, although the three-company garrison still lived in tents. The Coyoteros claimed almost 6,000 persons including 1,500 warriors under four principal chiefs: *Eskelthestsla* or *"Capitan Grande,"* Miguel, Pedro and *Capitan Chiquito.* These chiefs professed to be at peace with the Whites, and increasingly dependent on rations and tool issues. Settlers elsewhere complained that Coyoteros to whom Col. Green issued munitions for hunting traded it to hostile Apaches, and that they continued their raids into Sonora and southern Arizona.

Planning for extension of the national policy of reserving lands for Indians, the Army had recommended boundaries for a proposed Apache reservation. On 31 January 1870, Engineer Major H. M. Robert transmitted through channels a description of proposed boundaries. The New Mexico-Arizona boundary formed the eastern limit; the south rim of Black Mesa formed the northern limit; a line through Sombrero Butte, the crest of the Apache Mountains and down Salt River to Pinal Creek formed the western limit; the crest of the mountains just north of the Gila River formed the southern limit.

By the winter of 1870, military authorities reckoned that they controlled some 2,000 Apaches, who were cutting wood and hay to sell to the Army, along with surplus maize the women raised despite killing frosts. Col. Green paid for hay with flour and received cleaner fodder cheaper than Anglo-American contractors supplied.

Publication of reports of mineral resources in Arizona Territory that could not be exploited profitably because of Indian hostilities, generated interest among politically powerful capitalists to end hostilities. President Grant appointed Vincent Colyer as special commissioner to negotiate with the Apaches. By 1871, final pacification of Western Apache bands seemed only a question of time and opportunity. The quality of Apache resistance to conquest may be guessed from rough totals: since 1862 the U. S. had spent about $38,000,000 to kill fewer than 100 Apaches (old men, women and children included), while losing over 1,000 troops and civilians. Still, numerical superiority wore down the wily western warriors, so the period was propitious for a peace mission.

After conferring with Colyer at Long Branch, New Jersey, in mid-July, 1871, the President enlarged the special commissioner's powers, and sent him off to the Southwest. Colyer braved open contempt and hostility of Anglo-Americans with vested interests in continued hostilities. He endured the skepticism of Army officers eager to keep decision-making in their own hands. He suffered the uncertainties of negotiation with Indians ignorant of his powers and mistrusting after experiencing years of Anglo-American conference perfidy. Yet Colyer carried out his presidential mission.

A Century of Reservation Life, 1871-1971

RESERVATION ESTABLISHED. While at Camp Apache on 5 September 1871, Commissioner Colyer formally notified Col. John Green that exercising his special powers, he selected the White Mountain Reservation set aside by Major General Thomas, acting for the War Department "as one of the Indian reservations upon which the Apache Indians of Arizona may be collected, fed, clothed, and otherwise provided for and protected. . ." Colyer made the practical suggestion that Green issue the Apaches one pound of beef and one pound of maize per person per day, with salt, and issue coffee and sugar "occasionally." While still in Santa Fe, Colyer had ordered $2,000 worth of maize, beef and clothing for these Apaches, for whom C. E. Cooley interceded. At Fort Apache, Colyer reconciled *Esketestla,* who fled with his people when he learned about the Camp Grant massacre, and Miguel, who had slain six of *Esketestla's* band to satisfy the Army.

When Colyer returned to Washington toward

the end of the year, he participated in a conference with the President on 6 November that laid down a federal policy for Apache affairs. President Grant agreed to create executive order Indian reservations in the areas Colyer selected. Indian groups were to be required to reside on those reservations, where they would receive rations as long as they remained friendly. Warriors and non-combatants alike had to stay on the reserves. The government would warn its non-Indian citizens that it would protect peaceful Indians to the limits of its power. The War Department would select discreet and otherwise suitable officers to act as Indian agents until civilian agents could be appointed.

The day after the conference, Commissioner Colyer notified the Secretary of the Interior which areas he had selected for Apache reservations, including the White Mountain military reserve for the Coyoteros of Arizona at Camp Apache. The Secretary formally endorsed Colyer's recommendations to the President that same day, and two days later President Grant ordered the Secretary of War to take such action as might be required to carry out the recommendations of the Interior Secretary. General W. T. Sherman that same day dispatched implementing orders to General J. M. Schofield, commanding the Military Division of the Pacific. Noting that peaceful Indians "should not be permitted to starve, and our experience is that the Indian Bureau is rarely supplied with the necessary money to provide food," Sherman authorized Schofield to draw supplies from his commissary department. He also admonished Schofield to have reservation boundaries clearly marked and to advise the Arizona citizenry of the Presidential decisions.

The Coyotero bands led by Alchesay, Miguel, Esketestsla, Pedro and Pitone cooperated in federal control measures on their reserve. Three weeks before Colyer's visit, Gen. George H. Crook enlisted a Coyotero Indian Scout company at Fort Apache, where he discharged Mexican scouts hired at Tucson. He suspended recruitment while Colyer was on the scene, but work as Indian Scouts became important in White Mountain Apache post-conquest economics. Although the reservation included their previous habitat, the people found that reservation life meant radical changes in their way of life. Government rations became necessities for survival. Maize growing, seed-gathering, hunting continued, but the people suffered for lack of animal protein from Mexican cattle and horses and game formerly killed outside the reserve, and for lack of mescal they dared not go to seek. Yet during the 1872 growing season, the White Mountain Apaches worked hard and sold over 80,000 pounds of maize and fodder at harvest time. Anglo-American purchases of such Indian production aimed toward prompt integration of

CHIEF ALCHESAY (center left) as a young man. The youth at Alchesay's feet is Baha, hereditary head chief who succeeded Alchesay. Top row right is reputedly "Toggy-Snoggy" and second from left possibly Eskahnadktah. Beside Alchesay appears Bylas, head of the White Mountain Apaches who remained on San Carlos Reservation, for whom the contemporary settlement of Bylas was named.

the White Mountain Apaches into the national economy. Such Indian integration policies outraged dollar-greedy Anglo-American pioneers who coveted supply contracts for both soldiers and Indians. Covetous contractors possessed more political "pull" than honest career Army officers trying to teach Apaches how to enter the market economy, or Indian agents who perceived Apaches as human beings. They long preserved their profits by supplying what Apaches themselves could have provided.

Even Army officers reputed to understand Western Apaches treated the White Mountain Bands with a heavy hand. Despite the horticultural industry of these Apaches, Crook ordered on 5 November 1872 that within ten days all Apache residents of Fort Apache reservation were to move within one mile of the fort and report for daily muster. He dispatched an Army captain to make a daily count. Any individual not complying was to be treated as a prisoner of war as Crook shifted to the offensive on 15 November. The people understandably displayed little enthusiasm for enlisting as Indian Scouts when a major arrived to recruit a few days after Crook's order. They had little motivation to leave their unharvested crops, scattered homes, or allow their livestock to stray. Federal authorities within a short time relaxed the order to allow White Mountain Apaches to range up to ten miles away from the post, but the basic harm had been done.

Crook himself visited Camp Apache to enlist more Indian Scouts at the end of the year, enrolling among others Nakaidoklinni, who became a key dissident nine years later, and Alchesay, who came to be considered hereditary head chief. Thus, federal officials accelerated termination of hostilities with Western Apaches by recruiting relatively peacefully inclined masters of guerrilla warfare to meet the remaining hostiles in the field. Thus Army officers set White Mountain Apaches as allies upon a different plane of inter-ethnic relationship than obtained between Anglo-Americans and hostile bands. General Crook singled out Alchesay for his services as a scout. Chief Alchesay held the rank of sergeant and won the Congressional Medal of Honor for bravery during the 1872-73 campaign, along with nine other scouts. The White Mountain Apache Company "A" commanded by Lt. Charles B. Gatewood helped to garrison Fort Apache until the Army demobilized most Indian scouts after 1886. A small Scout unit of White Mountain Apaches remained on duty until 1943.

SOCIAL AND ECONOMIC UPSETS. Pacification and restriction to a reservation and later a tiny fraction thereof, produced serious longterm problems for White Mountain Apaches. First, pacification brought immediate and severe economic depression to all Western Apaches. Prohibited from raiding and kept under tight Army surveillance that prohibited trading, these Indians had no available economic alternatives. The pre-pacification standard of living plummeted as virtually every adult male was thrown out of work. While men could still hunt, the Army interdicted hunting outside the boundaries of the reservation or even smaller military mustering areas, and frowned on hunting parties spending time away from Army vigilance. There was little left for Apache men to do but to gamble with buckskin or horsehide replicas of Spanish playing cards, to drink *tulapai* or stronger alcoholic beverages, a taste for which they had acquired in the bars of Spanish frontier garrisons, grumble and grouse and fight among themselves, seek solace from their wives, stand around and stare at the conquerors, or join the Indian Scouts.

Internment not only idled most men, it also forcibly changed clothing styles. Women traditionally tanned buckskins to fashion into tunics, breechclouts and caps for the men and short skirts and waist-length tunics open at the sides for themselves. They made high-topped buckskin moccasins for everyone. Well-to-do families bordered their moccasins and clothing with decorative porcupine quills, and women liked to sew small bells or brass tinklers on their skirts. Men sported shell, feather or skin earrings while

ELDERLY WHITE MOUNTAIN APACHE WOMAN wearing the style camp costume conservative women usually wore when no Whites were around.

women fashioned necklaces and bracelets from antelope or deer hooves, shells, fish spines, and aromatic plant roots. When the Army restricted hunting, it so reduced the buckskin supply as to force the White Mountain Apaches to adopt different materials to clothe themselves as their buckskins wore out. Western Apache women emulated Mexican peasant women's clothes. They took fifteen to twenty yards of brightly colored sateen or percale to make a very full ankle length skirt with a deep flounce and numerous rows of decorative braid parallel to the hem. They made hip-length high-necked blouses hanging from a smooth yoke, full-sleeved and unbelted. Western Apache seamstresses utilized either prints or plain colored scarlet, blue, green, purple or orange cloth. As late as the turn of the century, some old women donned a blouse only when Whites appeared. After a period of dependence upon Army surplus clothing, Western Apache men donned blue denim jeans and brightly hued cotton shirts, completing their cowboy look with a broad-brimmed Stetson. During long poverty-stricken years, poorer Apaches covered themselves with little more than rags.

Internment also altered housing. Army hunting prohibitions forever ended the Plains style tipi among these people. They substituted canvas or grass thatching like that of their erstwhile Northern Piman enemies to create

APACHE SQUAW WITH HER NOSE CUT OFF FOR ADULTERY. 3.

Courtesy Arizona Historical Society

WHITE MOUNTAIN APACHE WOMAN whose nose-tip was cut off as punishment for adultery, real or presumed.

shelter, always poor in non-Indian eyes. Nor did Apache housekeeping impress Anglo-Americans as sanitary.

White Mountain Apache men not only lost their standing as meat and skin providers, but also their traditional rights to thrash their wives and cut off their nose tips for adultery. Anglo-American military and civil authorities displayed their own cultural biases in prohibiting both customs.

LAND LOSSES. While the White Mountain Apaches tried to carry out the cultural revolution required for rapid adjustment to survival as a conquered ethnic minority, Washington officialdom played ducks and drakes with Western Apache lands. On 14 December 1872, President Grant restored the Camp Grant Reservation to the public domain while establishing a Chiricahua Reservation in southeastern Arizona. At the same time, he enlarged White Mountain Reservation by adding a "San Carlos Division." This comprised an area fifteen miles south of the Gila River from New Mexico to the line through the Pinal Mountain crest.

Later Anglo-American pressures influenced the President progressively to diminish the area reserved for the White Mountain Apaches. On 21 July 1874, Grant returned to the public domain a great corridor between New Mexico and 109 degrees 30 minutes west longitude. Anglo-American corporations quickly developed very

46

profitable mines in this area at Clifton and Morenci.

FORCED RELOCATION. An initial relatively easy transition from isolated pre-conquest life to post-conquest reservation conditions ended for some 1,800 Coyoteros in 1875. Inevitable conflicts between military and civil officials at Fort Apache brought orders for the Coyoteros to move to San Carlos. The Captain commanding Fort Apache had forcibly occupied the Agency. Telegraphod by the ousted agent, the Commissioner of Indian Affairs ordered John P. Clum to take charge, which he did with 50 Apaches from San Carlos. Ordered to Washington for a conference, Clum urged removal of Fort Apache. The Commissioner instead told Clum to move the Coyoteros. Eight Coyotero bands that formerly gardened on the Gila River near Fort Goodwin readily acceeded to moving. Seven other northern bands hesitated. Nonetheless, Clum led the hesitant bands and interpreter George H. Stevens led the other eight comprising over 1,000 Coyoteros to hot, arid San Carlos. Arriving on 31 July 1875, they encountered Arivaipa, Tonto and Chiricahua Apaches and Yavapais. Some Coyoteros remained in their own territory, since the chiefs and many members of three bands were Indian Scouts stationed at Fort Apache. Chief Diablo, saying his band would prefer death to removal, obtained permission to stay. Half the Carrizo

Band that sought refuge in Diablo's band territory prior to 1855 evidently stayed with him. By 1878, over 5,000 Western Apaches and Yavapais were concentrated at San Carlos.

The White Mountain Apaches forced to relocate to San Carlos came under the administration of a moral, energetic and sympathetic young Indian Agent. Clum managed the daily roll and relegated the Army to reservation border patrol and pursuit of runaway Indians after 9 October 1875. Establishing an Indian police force, he required the various Indian groups to select their own policemen who were responsible for dealing with the Agent and maintaining order. Clum also set up a court with native judges. After Clum brought most of the Coyoteros to San Carlos, he expanded his Indian police force from eight to 25 men, adding a number of Coyoteros.

Convinced that the ration system harmed the Apaches, Clum paid scrip redeemable for goods at the agency store to able-bodied Indians he put to work building roads, irrigation works and buildings. Clum valiantly attempted to enforce federal legislation prohibiting alcoholic beverages to Indians. He also led a group of Western Apache chiefs on a tour to Washington, staging a series of Wild West shows. Coyotero Chief Diablo took along his young son.

The government purchased scrawny range cattle from pioneer Anglo-American cattlemen

48

to provide Apaches with meat, yet did little or nothing to encourage Indians who had introduced stolen Mexican cattle onto the Apachería pastures to build up herds to feed themselves or to sell. The government purchased white flour, sugar, coffee and tea from White suppliers. Pumping tax funds into the dominant group's economic system to ration suddenly dependent Apaches created strong vested interests in keeping them dependent. No federal action instituted a scheme for paying massively unemployed Apaches to grow wheat or maize or other commercial crops to subsist these defeated people. No one widened Clum's arrangement of recompensing public works labor in scrip redeemable in goods. Thus, rationing perpetuated Apache unemployment and postponed integration of Western Apaches into the national market as producers rather than welfare recipients. Whatever game Apaches killed, whatever wild foods they found and whatever crops they nursed from the soil, they obtained almost in spite of federal supervision.

In fact, continued disputes with military officers over these and other issues led Clum to resign in 1877 to fight for Apache rights as a private citizen. Yet his influence on U. S. Indian administration spread far even after he resigned. His demonstration of the value of Apache responsibility for maintaining order inspired a national Indian police system. Congress on 27

May 1878 passed an act authorizing organization of Indian police. The Bureau of Indian Affairs urged adopting the plan on all major reservations, and within two years 84 officers and 746 policemen served on 40 agencies.

Coyotero Apaches moved to San Carlos had contributed to Clum's demonstration that Apaches vested with responsibility acted responsibly. When Chiricahuas left their reservation and returned to the warpath in the spring of 1876, Clum challenged the Indians concentrated at San Carlos to prove their steadfastness. Those Apaches volunteered to fight the hostiles and within six hours of Clum's return to the reservation from Tucson with news of the situation, 250 men rode into the agency. After drilling his volunteers and providing them with rations, Clum waited two weeks before the Commissioner of Indian Affairs ordered him to take charge of the Chiricahua Agency and remove those Apaches to San Carlos. A week later, Clum rode to Tucson leading a select force of 54 Arivaipa and Coyotero Apaches. These Indians readily persuaded the Chiricahuas to settle at San Carlos. The White Mountain Apaches proved again their basic peacefulness and determination to adjust to living in a country dominated by Anglo-Americans.

They did so despite continued United States seizure of their ancestral lands. Early in 1876, prospectors discovered rich silver deposits at

Globe, Arizona, within the reservation. On 27 April, President Grant redefined the western boundary of Fort Apache reservation as a line due south from Black Mesa to Sombrero Butte, then southeast to Chromo Peak and then south to the mouth of the San Pedro River. Again, Anglo-American entrepreneurs soon developed profitable mines in this region. On 26 January 1877, President Grant removed 7,421 acres surveyed by Lt. E. D. Thomas from Fort Apache reservation.

At that period, approximately 500 of the Coyoteros relocated on San Carlos Reservation lived near modern Bylas. The Indians were so crowded that they dared to express discontent. Even on the reservation, White Mountain Apaches lost property to renegade raiders such as Victorio in 1877. Then the Army interned 169 of his Warm Springs Band at Fort Apache.

RETURN TO HOMELAND. When Victorio took the warpath again in the autumn of 1879, White Mountain Apache Scouts in Company "A" pursued his band. Possibly their performance decided federal officials in 1879 that some dispersion of Western Apaches concentrated at San Carlos could be allowed. About 500 Coyoteros returned to the Fort Apache region after four years of internment in foreign territory. In succeeding years, more Coyoteros obtained permission to return northward to their historic ranges, including the Cibecue Band. The

51

latter found their reservation range being invaded from the west by Mormon and other Anglo-American settlers.

Under these psychological stresses, many of the Cibecue Band joined in a messianic movement that led to open violence in 1881. A renowned Cibecue Band medicine man named Nakaidoklinni who reportedly journeyed to Washington in 1871 and wore a Presidential medal, agreed to restore to life two White Mountain Band war leaders, Diablo and Eskiole. They reportedly killed one another while drunk on *tulapai.* Nakaidoklinne's ritual generated considerable religious excitement. Failing to bring the two back to life, Nakaidoklinni preached that his life-restoring power could work only if all White were destroyed. He began a new dance in which files of people moved like spokes in a wheel, with the prophet at the hub. As Nakaidoklinni led ceremonies at Carrizo and near Fort Apache designed to make an end with the Whites, Apache excitement mounted. Indian policemen sent to request that Nakaidoklinni report to the San Carlos Agency were disarmed at a Cibecue dance. The Indian agent demanded that troops arrest Nakaidoklinni. Colonel E. A. Carr attempt to carry out the order with 79 cavalrymen and 23 Apache Scouts. His command took Nakaidoklinni into custody without resistance. Nakaidoklinni expressed readiness to go, saying he did not come earlier because he was treating a patient. Carr later reported that White Mountain Apaches attacked the cavalrymen as they camped that evening. All but a few of the Indian Scouts deserted. Three were later court martialed and hung. According to Carr's orders, a sergeant in charge of the prisoner shot him. Nakaidoklinni's son reportedly rode up to receive a mortal wound, and his wife was shot in self-defense by a trooper she assertedly tried to kill. Although Nakaidoklinni's followers sent runners to Fort Apache to announce that Carr was slain, several hundred Apaches failed to press home their advantage. The cavalrymen slipped away during the night, reaching Fort Apache the next afternoon. Outraged Apaches killed four Mormons and three soldiers in isolated areas, and fired on the post. Twenty-two companies mobilized to meet the "threat" and the troops and their mounts dealt recovering White Mountain Apache horticulture a heavy blow by consuming the produce of many fields in which they camped.

Massive troop movements frightened the recently settled anti-White Chiricahua Band faction led by Geronimo. It fled to link up with the Warm Springs chief Victorio in Mexico. Thus the Army obtained hostile Apaches off-reservation once again to justify a large Indian-fighting force continuing in the Southwest. Federal authorities once again forced relocation inside a "peace line." Five chiefs and 60 lesser leaders surrendered. Moved to Fort Grant under guard, they eventually won acquittal except for five Scouts judged to have mutinied. One wonders whether even those Scouts simply reacted in outrage when cavalrymen adopted the Mexican "law of flight" to dispose of Nakaidoklinni after his arrest.

Participants in the Nakaidoklinni movement attacked San Carlos in July, 1882, killing its police chief. Nantiatish, a Cibecue Band leader, failed to organize a general revolt. Settlers repulsed his half a hundred when they attacked McMillenville, and troops virtually wiped out his party in the Mogollon Rim country in the last major action between hostile Apaches and U. S. forces in Arizona.

Peace reigned on Fort Apache Reservation from 1882 with the Army under General Crook in complete charge. This meant military discipline along with prohibition, although Crook allowed dispersed settlement. Geronimo with his followers settled on Turkey Creek after their 1883 surrender. Crook encouraged Coyoteros to return to Fort Apache Reservation, so 900 did soon after he assumed command. The government also issued 700 head of cattle and encouraged Apaches to raise stock. Army officers and Bureau of Indian Affairs officials squabled again in 1885. Geronimo's Chiricahuas brewed *tulapai* from the first maize they had grown in years, despite Crook's prohibition policy, locally enforced by Lt. Britton Davis. Seething at previous imprisonment of a man they believed two interpreters framed, and outraged by an officer who drank having the gall to lecture them against drinking homebrew, 130 to 140 Chiricahuas fled once again with Geronimo leading. Evading a massive Army manhunt, the Chiricahua-Warm Springs fighters raced to Mexico. Late in November a party returned to Fort Apache to kill the reservation cattle herders, steal Bonito's horses and carry off several women. When General Nelson A. Miles visited Fort Apache in July, 1886, he labeled the Chiricahuas and Warm Springs Apaches still there the most "turbulent, desperate, disreputable band of human beings" he had ever seen. Some 400 of them grew enough maize on 100 acres to hold a *tulapai* party every night, firing off their arms while in "drunken orgies."

When Apache Scouts brought the renegades to bay in Mexico, White Mountain Chief Alchesay and Chiricahua Kaentena, specially released from Alcatraz, negotiated Geronimo's surrender, aborted when the hostile leader got drunk. When troops under General Miles obtained Geronimo's next surrender in Mexico, his group was exiled to Florida along with Chiricahuas remaining on Fort Apache Reservation. President Theodore Roosevelt selected Fort Marion as the spot where not only the renegade but also the peaceful Chiricahua and Warm

Springs survivors on Turkey Creek would be interned as "prisoners of war." Instructing Colonel J. F. Wade, in command of Fort Apache, how to round up these people, General Miles "watched" the operation from the sanctuary of the Wilcox telegraph office 200 miles south.

Once the cavalry removed the Chirichuas and Warm Springs Band remnant, some 2,000 White Mountain and Cibecue Band Apaches continued their hunting, food collecting and gardening, still very dependent upon rations. They remained peaceful, but poverty-stricken. Textiles, hats, metal tools and utensils all required cash. In 1891, the federal government still purchased 500,000 pounds of beef from an Anglo-American contractor to ration the White Mountain people.

Twenty years after the White Mountain Reservation was set apart, Congress continued to reduce its area. On 20 February 1893, Congress approved an act to restore to the public domain an area around the McMillen mine camp, extending a few miles along Salt River at the western margin of the reserved area. Congress did provide that proceeds from sales of these lands were to be held in trust for Indians on the reserve after survey costs were paid. On the other hand, it stated that nothing in the act should be construed as recognizing Indian ownership of the reserve.

Not until 1897 did the federal government clarify the administrative distinction between Fort Apache Reservation and San Carlos Reservation. Since 1881, Army officers administered the combined jurisdiction as agents, and the 1890 four-company garrison at Fort Apache (plus five at San Carlos) represented Army estimates of the force it required in peacetime! In 1897 separation came by act of Congress labeling reserved lands north of Black River as the "Fort Apache Reservation" with headquarters at the post. That action insulated White Mountain Apaches from the problems of multi-tribal adjustment on San Carlos Reservation. It also set the stage for reservation-wide self-government forty years later, after a period of social transformation of historic bands into settlements. Soldiers stationed at Fort Apache and businessmen entering the region contributed to wider social integration by marrying Apache wives. They set new styles of housing, and Apache families began to erect frame houses as they abandoned the funeral custom of burning a hut in which anyone died.

At the end of federal policy shifts, Fort Apache Reservation contained 1,664,872 acres, of which 1,657,451 acres were tribally controlled and 7,421 reserved for the government. Later, when the Bureau of Indian Affairs leased range to Anglo-American cattle growers and sold timber cutting privileges to Anglo-American corporations, Congress all too often appropriated monies they paid to defray the costs of federal administration. Instead of appropriating tax revenues to pay bureaucratic salaries, purchase automobiles, gas, trucks, machinery, etc., Congressmen happily appropriated "tribal" funds. Thus, even after reservation lands began to earn cash income, Congress did not allow White Mountain Apaches to benefit directly from it, except for three or four miniscule per capita payments. When the great economic depression struck, Congress actually appropriated "tribal" funds until none remained!

AGENCY TOWN. Whiteriver developed as reservation administrative community for Fort Apache Reservation after deactivation of Fort Apache. It became the main focus of contacts with officials of the U. S. government, with the "cozy cottages" of Bureau of Indian Affairs employees and government buildings surrounded by a fringe of sun-bleached, smoke-blackened native huts. Whiteriver had three traders by World War II. In 1971, Whiteriver's suburbs boast the newest and most elegant Apache housing. The White Mountain Apache Housing Authority joined with the Tribal Council, Bureau of Indian Affairs, U. S. Public Health Service, and would-be home owners to create three outlying subdivisions. North Whiteriver contains 63 mutual help homes, with 16 more and a community center at Diamond Creek four

58

Courtesy Arizona Historical Society

TEMPORARY HOUSING for a White Mountain Apache family off Fort Apache Reservation about 1888. This is the transitional style dwelling now being rapidly replaced by modern frame houses erected through the mutual help housing program.

miles north. Closer to the center of town, older plank homes are still occupied, often supplemented with a brush-covered hut or shade during the summer. The Tribe erected 35 rental homes at the southwest edge of town, and 20 rental units put up by the sawmill stand between it and downtown Whiteriver.

The number of Bureau of Indian Affairs and other federal employees increased through the years. By 1931, the Bureau employed 73 persons locally, 23 of them Apaches. Typically better educated than other tribesmen, Apache employees tended to move to live in Whiteriver, where the largest public school for White Mountain Apaches was built, and the first public high school opened.

Although former Commissioner of Indian Affairs John Collier instituted preferential hiring of Indians, Indian domination of Bureau posts appears to lie in the future. Even under a superintendent quite sympathetic to White Mountain Apaches, only 46 worked for the Whiteriver agency in 1962, compared to 83 Anglo-Americans. This meant only a slight increase in proportion of Apache employees from 31 percent in 1931 to 35 percent in 1962. By 1971, the Bureau claimed that Indians constituted 57 percent of its 133 Fort Apache Agency employees.

Despite emergence of Whiteriver as the reservation's major population center, economic pursuits keep much of the population scattered. While White Mountain Apaches maintain clan affiliation, they have developed localized residence groups in place of bands. These perform the same function as bands in adjusting population to reservation resources. North Fork, Canyon Day, East Fork and Turkey Creek all lie within a 10-mile radius of Whiteriver. Largest rural settlement is Cibecue with some 350 families, a sawmill started in 1965, a community building dating from 1963, two schools, five Christian churches and two trading posts. Like Carrizo and Cedar Creek, Cibecue occupies an isolated western valley. The Tribal mutual help housing program has not overlooked these settlements. Canyon Day boasts 19 mutual help houses. Cedar Creek has 17 units while much more isolated Cibecue completed 30 and Carrizo five. Other program participants are finishing 10 homes at the edge of McNary.

CHRISTIANIZATION. While the Spanish government financed Christian missionaries among pagan Indians, it really did not attempt to convert Apaches. U. S. President Grant encouraged missionaries to convert conquered tribesmen. Yet Army officers prevented a Catholic missionary attempt immediately after pacification of the Western Apaches by denying material support. Nevertheless, a century of reservation life has ended White Mountain Apache war and hunting rites and ceremonies concerned with travel, horticulture and even childbirth.

Not until 25 years after Fort Apache was founded did Lutherans take up the challenge of converting White Mountain Apaches. The first missionary pitched his tent alongside the road from Fort Apache to East Fork in 1896. Three pioneer missionaries accomplished little until E. E. Guenther and his wife arrived in 1911. In time, they learned to speak Athapascan, while the Apaches learned more English. The Guenthers started the first orphanage for Indian children in the Southwest, starting with a spare room in an expanded parsonage. For many years unwanted twins (traditional Apache culture condemned one twin to death) comprised a major class of orphans. Even U. S. Public Health Service responsibility for Indian health fails to relieve the Lutherans of this responsibility which they still fund at an annual current cost of $65,000.

After Guenther hired assistants and moved to Whiteriver as superintendent of Lutheran missions on both Fort Apache and San Carlos Reservations, he built a new church dedicated in 1923. Chief Alchesay presided over opening the new church door, then led 100 Apaches to the altar for baptism, significantly accelerating the conversion rate. In time, E. E. Guenther turned leadership of Lutheran missions over to his son, Arthur. By the time E. E. Guenther died in 1961, the Lutherans counted congregations at

Whiteriver, Canyon Day, Cedar Creek, Carrizo, McNary, Maverick and two Cibecue locations. They operated a boarding school enrolling over 250 students with a waiting list.

Lutherans enjoyed the advantage of a monopoly on proselytizing during a quarter-century. Apaches convinced that the White man's religion must be powerful naturally became Lutherans, but often in a nominal way. Since 1921, additional denominations entered into competition for White Mountain Apache converts. Inevitably, they "steal" Apache "sheep" from the nominally Lutheran flock.

Roman Catholics first challenged the Lutheran monopoly in 1921. By the beginning of World War II, nearly all White Mountain Apaches had been influenced by one denomination or the other. Lutherans enjoyed approximately a nine to one advantage in numbers.

After the war, more denominations entered the competition and drastically altered religious conditions. An Assembly of God revivalist conducting services in Globe felt a call to minister to Apaches, and pitched his tent beside Whiteriver. Returned veterans and discharged war workers found total immersion, speaking in tongues and miraculous healing claims appealing in post-war social and economic confusion. The Whiteriver Assembly of God claims 206 members in 1971, and the denomination has expanded to Canyon Day, Cedar Creek, Cibecue, Carrizo and McNary.

In 1950, a Prescott stonemason felt called to extend Baptist beliefs to White Mountain Apaches. In 1956, he personally erected a church and parsonage. Another missionary and his wife have led this church north of Whiteriver all but five years since 1956. An Apache, Edgar Perry, serves the congregation of 115 as associate pastor.

The Church of Jesus Christ of Latter Day Saints entered the reservation in the 1950's with its young missionaries. Much of its effort centers upon recruiting bright Apache students to attend off-reservation Mormon schools.

The decade of the seventies has already witnessed further proliferation of sects. The Miracle Church leads current re-alignment of Apache denominational allegiance. It rapidly gained adherants although its missionary work was long conducted largely on payday weekends between May and September. The emotional appeal of the Miracle Church to White Mountain people lies in emphasis on miraculous cures. A key convert in this movement appears to be a young man who recovered from severe burns after two of his companions in a Jeep struck by a truck died. His father leads the Canyon Day Miracle Church. Other congregations exist in East Fork and Seven-Mile, and converts meet in homes on North Fork.

64

As ever more sects gain White Mountain
Apache followers, the Lutherans concentrate
upon strengthening congregational governance.
This means increased Apache financial and
moral responsibility. It puts Apache teachers in
vacation Bible schoolrooms. It involves Apache
men and women in nail-pulling bees to salvage
lumber donated to construct classrooms, and
raising funds to buy a bus.

Itinerant preachers frequently pass through
Fort Apache Reservation and criticize the
permanently installed denominations. Thus, the
Indians have for some years recognized that
White people are far from united upon their own
religion. Contemporary White Mountain
Apaches are, therefore, less convinced of the
power of Christianity than were their grand-
parents immediately after conquest when no
Christians carried their message to still-hated
former enemies. Consequently, many Apaches
today turn to traditional beliefs for solace.
Indeed, many have maintained some native faith
throughout a century of reservation life.

HOLY GROUND MOVEMENT. While Christian
missionaries have gained numerous White Mountain Apache converts, native religious leaders
have started at least two Apache sects. During
the stressful period 1903-1907, four White
Mountain Apache religious leaders belonging to
two closely related clans, conducted another
millenarian movement. Daslahdn, a Cibecue

medicine man, started the *dahgodiy'ah* or "They Will Be Raised Up" movement, teaching people to dance wearing white clothing and silver jewelry. The movement ended when Daslahdn and the cult leaders at Cedar Creek and Fort Apache died. Their deaths frightened people and the fourth leader who renamed his followers deserted his wife to remarry.

Another Fort Apache native, Silas John Edwards, began to cure a number of diseases after his 1921 vision of climbing a rainbow to receive God's instruction. He held a special power over snakes he employed in his ceremonies along with the cross. He taught his followers a ritual that combined both native Apache and Christian elements he learned as a member of a Catholic congregation earlier. He established "Holy Grounds" which gave their name to the movement. These rectangular areas are marked with crosses colored white on the north, green on the south, black on the east and yellow on the west. These color-direction associations are traditional among Apaches. Holy Ground ritual incorporated numerous other native elements, including singing in Athapascan to water-drum accompaniment and use of pollen and colored hoops, and creating colored ground paintings. Processions apparently reflect Christian influence.

Christian missionaries openly opposed the Holy Ground movement. Indian leaders appealed to the Bureau of Indian Affairs, which followed the Constitutional doctrine of freedom of religion. The movement spread to both Arizona Apache reservations and Fort McDowell and Camp Verde Yavapais during the 1920's. Convicted of murdering his wife in 1933, Silas John received a long jail sentence. Followers often visited him in prison to be healed. They maintained the Holy Ground cult until his release in 1954, when he reassumed the role of prophet. So great was his power that it slew "shooting witches" so White Mountain Apaches believe shooting sorcery is no longer practiced. Aware of Christian opposition, members of the Holy Ground movement celebrated their general summer rites far from Whiteriver and discouraged Anglo-American attendance.

In sum, whether Tucson oral tradition of Coyotero participation in church construction in Spanish times be correct or not, White Mountain Apaches have demonstrated great concern over religion during the reservation period, generating millenarian movements in 1881, 1903 and 1921 in addition to joining progressively more Pentecostal Christian sects stressing miraculous curing.

EDUCATION. For a score of years after Fort Apache Reservation was created, its people learned about U. S. society as their ancestors learned about colonial Spanish society. They picked up limited knowledge of the totality by observing occurrences at Fort Apache. They could see only military activities of the cavalry and a few employees of the Bureau of Indian Affairs holding authority over them. Neither accurately represented national society.

Although a few children attended boarding schools earlier, not until 1892 did the federal government establish the first school for White Mountain Apache children in a vacant Fort Apache barrack. Then it was a denominational school. Having no previous experience with formal classroom education, Apache parents and children did not understand what might be gained from formal instruction. Indian Service officials, the police and even the Army's Indian Scouts had to coerce 30 boys into attending the first school.

When the U. S. cavalry finally withdrew in 1922, it turned Fort Apache over to the Indian Bureau to use as a school. The Bureau was then facing pressing problems of providing classrooms for Navajos. It therefore devoted most of the school's capacity to educating Navajo rather than Apache students. The student body of 440 in 1931, for example, included only some 60 Apaches. The Bureau then enrolled 380 Apache students, however, at White River Boarding School. It operated two-grade day schools only at Cibecue and Canyon Day. The Lutherans operated a day school on East Fork with an average 53 pupils, another at Cibecue with 32, and an East Fork Boarding School attended by

32 pupils. A total of 756 White Mountain Apache children was enrolled in government, mission, and public schools.

After the Indians organized reservation-wide government in 1938, the tribal council made school attendance compulsory for children between six and eighteen. School bus drivers served as truant officers. By 1952, about 80 percent of Arizona's Apaches reportedly spoke English. Yet nearly all children still enter school from Athapascan-speaking homes on Fort Apache Reservation.

By 1958, approximately 1,500 White Mountain Apache children attended school. As population increased, in 1967 enrollment reached 2,100 students and in 1971 it was 2,600. The White Mountain Apache Tribe provided college scholarships for ten high school graduates in 1962, while it had 65 students in college in 1971.

In one reaction against White domination, the White Mountain Apaches are moving to preserve some of their own cultural heritage by teaching it with Anglo-American techniques. For example, a descendent of an Apache Scout directs a Culture Center housed in an old Fort Apache log cabin dating from 1875. The Tribal Council began funding this Center in 1969. Its collections include taped interviews with elder tribesmen, genealogies, an Apache dictionary and historic costumes. The staff jokingly refers to it as the "medicine man's house," and it indeed displays much ritual paraphernalia.

Since 1956, recreation program income has financed a summer youth camp that trains high school boys in conservation and range management.

MEDICINE. Traditional Western Apache religion concerned itself with the well-being of people in all activities. After a century of reservation life, only the female puberty rite, diagnostic and curing ceremonies survive. Not more than two dozen medicine men practice, Cibecue having the most with five.

Army physicians provided some medical services while Fort Apache was garrisoned. Officers expressed concern over high infant mortality rates. In the late 1920's, White Mountain Apaches pooled their own individual funds to raise $45,000 to construct a 60-bed hospital since Congress had not appropriated funds for such a facility. Tuberculosis then constituted a major health threat. Drinking *tulapai* also contributed to health problems by generating fights and murders.

Prostitution in the company lumber mill town of McNary reportedly spread venereal disease among White Mountain Apache workers in the mid-1920's.

When the U. S. Public Health Service assumed responsibility for Indian health in 1955, the Fort Apache Reservation death rate ran 20 per

A WHITE MOUNTAIN APACHE MOTHER with her infant on a cradleboard, taken in the 1800's. Carrying babies on the cradleboard was equivalent to swaddling them, and Apache women lined their cradleboards with soft, absorbent plant bark performing the same functions as diapers.

1,000 population, considerably higher than rates among Anglo-Americans. Children revealed 40 percent positive reaction to tuberculosis testing. Enteritis and diarrhea cases numbered nearly 300 annually, with 23 deaths during one sample year, 20 of them infants less than a year old. So serious is this problem still that the National Institute of Arthritis and Metabolic Disease has contracted with Johns Hopkins University to develop practical methods for treating acute diarrhea cases at Whiteriver Hospital.

In 1960, Whiteriver Hospital had a rated capacity of 38 beds, and handled over 150 patients per month. In 1971, the U. S. Public Health Service hospital had been augmented to a 52-bed rated capacity.

Today, most White Mountain Apaches promptly take their ills to the reservation medical staff for diagnosis and treatment. Only those who fail to obtain quick relief for their symptoms there resort to native curers.

ECONOMIC INTEGRATION. Early Army prohibitions on hunting, raiding and wild food collecting, Agent Clum's system of paying for work in scrip redeemable in goods, General Crook's wood and hay purchase policy, and later experience working for wages converted White Mountain Apaches into consumer participants in the national market. By World War II, Fort Apache Reservation sustained not only three traders at Whiteriver, but others at Cibecue, Carrizo, Cedar

Creek and Fort Apache. The principal limitation upon reservation contributions to the national economy continued to be the marginality of Apaches as producers.

Favored by a food-rich mountain habitat, the people survived the great depression of the 1930's consuming as many wild foods, probably, as any Indian group in the U. S. Acorns, pinyon nuts and walnuts provided valuable nutrients. One yucca species yielded a delicious fruit. People continued eating mesquite pods, wild onions and potatoes, pit-roasted agave hearts, and brewed medicinal teas from sycamore bark and numerous other plants. Poverty in terms of cash being a permanent reservation condition until that time, most White Mountain Apaches cooked over open outdoor fires with few purchased utensils. Most families owned Dutch ovens, ideal for cooking maize bread, beans and meat. A skillet fried tortillas of wheat, maize or acorn meal, or pulverized jerky mixed with onions, hot peppers or hominy.

While continued utilization of wild foods helped people weather economic depression, other customs fostered the appearance, if not the reality, of poverty. If the Apaches did not already possess a strong fear of souls of dead persons, historic experience with epidemic diseases generated the practice of burning the home of one who died. This custom fostered a lingering preference for living in huts that required little capital investment. Late in the 1920's, however, the Bureau of Indian Affairs permitted Fort Apache Agency to allow Indian families $300 worth of lumber from the local sawmill. Over 75 frame houses sprang up in the first couple of years under this policy. By World War II, families living in Anglo-American style houses simply abandoned them for a period if someone died inside, rather than burning them down. Conversion of White Mountain Apaches to Christian denominations with a different concept of the soul has fundamentally influenced attitudes toward housing. The brightly painted, two to five bedroom mutual help houses built in recent years attest to the radical change in belief and shelter.

A decade ago, only a quarter of the adult men were regularly employed, the rest finding only part-time jobs or receiving public assistance. Income averaged only some $900 annually, and had still to be eked out with hunting, collecting wild foods and gardening. Expansion of employment in tribal enterprises since then has helped improve the reservation economy, yet the increase in population adds workers to the labor force about as fast as new jobs are created.

LIVESTOCK INDUSTRY. Apache stockmen who grazed war booty cattle from Mexico in their mountain fastnesses prior to conquest could not maintain herds through the early post-conquest period. Forced relocation of some

74

1,600 people at San Carlos almost guaranteed that. A few Coyoteros may have started herds with some of the 200 cows, 200 goats and 200 donkeys that Agent Clum purchased for his combined Western Apache charges in 1875. A few families drew live animals at the weekly beef ration and saved them to build small herds. One had 384 head by 1884. A cattle issue of 700 head that year started more White Mountain Apaches in cattle husbandry.

Indians expanding their cattle herds faced stiff grazing competition from Anglo-American stockmen who leased from the Bureau of Indian Affairs much of the northern and western parts of Fort Apache Reservation. These ranchers found leasing the best grazing lands to be one way to despoil Indian resources they could not obtain by purchase. They turned thousands of head of unregistered cattle on the reservation range, seriously overgrazing it. Moreover, Apaches sold over 200 tons of hay per year well into this century, further depleting the grasses.

In 1917, the federal government established a 400-head Indian Department herd on Fort Apache Reservation, and started 80 Apache families in the cattle business by issuing each five head. Leasing pasturage to Whites continued for another decade, however, until Superintendent William Donner arrived in 1927. He ended leasing when the last agreement expired in 1932. Donner encouraged each Apache youth ready for marriage to raise cattle by issuing him a few head, assigning him a brand, and providing him with technical assistance. By 1931, Indians ran 20,000 head of cattle on Fort Apache Reservation. Two major difficulties occurred in herd quality improvement. Most Apaches valued horses more than cattle, so grazed them at the expense of cattle. Liking good beef, Apaches tended to slaughter their best heifers and calves, especially those that strayed from one group's range onto that of another. Sales brought in $132,411 to 580 families that owned from five to 1,800 head in 1931. There were at that time 650 families in all. The tribal herd then numbered 2,200 head.

Well-trained Bureau of Indian Affairs technicians ensured effective stock improvement. The Bureau obtained 400 purebred cattle in 1934 to provide bulls to family stock raisers willing to upbreed their animals. This herd was augmented with 390 purebred heifers in 1938. Thus, the Hereford cattle owned by the various cattle associations operating in eight reservation grazing districts reached high quality by mid-century. The White Mountain Apache range cattle industry grossed approximately $1,000,000 annually between 1945 and 1951. Then prices fell precipitously, so sales dropped from $818,000 in 1951 to $447,469 in 1954.

During that period, technicians persuaded stock owners to reduce the number of animals

Western Ways Photograph by Charles W. Herbert

CATTLE ROUND-UP on the Fort Apache Reservation, showing a water hole created to open additional high altitude meadow as pasturage for the high quality Herefords grown by the White Mountain Apaches.

grazed from 21,510 owned by 800 families in 1944 to a low of 14,568 owned by 522 families in 1952. Only seven families then owned the 100 head or more considered to be adequate to support a family, while 693 families owned no cattle at all. Thereafter, cattle numbers rose slowly so that by 1962, stockmen were running 17,000 head.

At fall roundup, all members of each cattle association ride when their animals are gathered and then driven to sorting pastures and auction pens where they are sold to the highest bidder. The sale drives usually occur early in October. In 1970, the fall auction realized some $780,000.

The tribal government maintains its herd of purebred registered Herefords on a tribal range of some 138,000 acres on the southeast corner of the reservation. A full-time manager supervised by a board of directors runs this as a model ranch to set an example for cattle owners, to raise breeding stock to sell to the cattle associations, and to produce tribal revenue through off-reservation sales.

LUMBERING. When President U. S. Grant reserved lands for the White Mountain Apaches, he set aside comparatively rich resources in modern terms. Fort Apache Reservation rises northward from a low of 2,700 feet above sea level along Black River Canyon to the 11,459 foot summit of Mt. Thomas. Winter snows at higher elevations provide abundant moisture for heavy stands of commercial timber. The White Mountains occupy about two-thirds of the reservation surface, and support both pine and aspen.

Apaches asked to be allowed to set up sawmills well before 1900. Yet commercial logging began only in 1920 after Thomas Pollack and his associates started building a mill and railroad in 1917. Hard times hit lumbermen soon thereafter. In the 1931 fiscal year, the White Mountain Apaches sold wood in cords for only $4,945. Government sawmills produced that year lumber worth $15,533, and one private company paid the tribe $105. Between 1917 and 1931, reservation lumber sold for $1,200,000 in total.

Lumber company officials operating under contracts requiring preferential Apache hiring "on equal terms" complained that they could not depend upon Apaches, so employed only about a fourth Apaches. An all-Apache crew feeding logs into the mill frequently shut it down by going home when a storm struck, so the company relied on ethnically mixed crews and attributed Apache behavior to lack of experience in industry, rather than rejection of the sort of subservience imported Negro workers displayed to managers.

As the lumber market recovered, Southwest Forest Products of McNary purchased from the Tribe about 65 percent of the annual cut, handled through its model logging camp at

Maverick and an extensive system of outlying camps. This corporation hired some 70 Apaches in the early 1960's because the Tribe insisted on employment preference for tribesmen by corporations doing business on the reservation. By that time, the U. S. was well recovered from its great depression, and lumbering was the major source of tribal operating income and capital to invest in job-creating development projects. By 1950, annual timber income reached $383,572, climbing to $472,400 in 1955, rising to $489,155 in 1960 to only $587,176 in 1965. In 1969, the White Mountain Apaches, having installed a tribal sawmill at Whiteriver, took in $1,725,822 from timber sales, up from $1,138,946 in 1968.

The new tribal sawmill at Whiteriver employs 100 persons and keeps 40 to 50 Apaches at work in the woods. The tribally owned Fort Apache Timber Company processes over 50,000,000 board feet annually. Thus, the White Mountain Apaches, with Bureau of Indian Affairs technical assistance, run a tribal timber business, and permit private enterprise.

CRAFTS. Before history, Apacheans necessarily produced all their own clothing, weapons, tools and utensils. The latter consisted of a few baked clay pots (displaced by metal long ago) gourd cups, skin bags, baskets, bone awls and stone grinding tools usually salvaged from prehistoric Pueblo ruins. Once they began raiding

80

WHITE MOUNTAIN APACHE BASKETMAKER twining a burden basket. A water jar waterproofed with pinyon pitch appears second from the right in the front row of baskets.

Spanish colonial settlements, Western Apaches obtained metal tools and utensils of all descriptions as spoils of war. Pacification a century ago plunged White Mountain Apaches into a subsistence-welfare economy. One traditional utensil found, however, an immediate market among non-Indians because of its beauty and utility. Twined and coiled basket sales provided women some cash income.

Large burden baskets and water jars are twined; the latter are also waterproofed with pinyon pitch. Basketmakers often decorated burden baskets with buckskin thongs and sometimes sewed trade beads on for additional decoration. Trays and bowls are made in coils sewn together from willow or cottonwood with black designs executed with tough outer skins from devil's claw seedpods. Although cash returns from basketry are low calculated hourly, some White Mountain Apache women still fashion fine baskets for sale through tribal stores. Sometimes a cradleboard maker will produce a cradleboard to sell to a non-Indian rather than an Apache mother, and others sell beadwork.

SELF-GOVERNMENT. Apparently much of the contemporary economic integration and social strength of the White Mountain Apache people stems from an exceptional quality leadership. Certainly a key chief during the cultural transition from band autonomy to reservation cooperation was Alchesay. Whatever his pre-conquest authority may have been, Alchesay quickly came to the fore. His gallantry in action as an Indian Scout non-commissioned officer, and his personal relationship with high-ranking officers, such as General George H. Crook, validated his credentials as head chief in Anglo-American eyes. Evidently their treatment of Alchesay reinforced his authority among his own people.

Alchesay admonished White Mountain Apaches to adjust to life under Anglo-American domination. Cavalry occupation until 1922 coupled with authoritarian superintendents deprived Alchesay and other native leaders of much power. Some men appointed "Tag-Band" chiefs were not trained as chiefs, weakening the pre-reservation leadership. Tag-band chiefs functioned as true leaders for a time, drawing and distributing rations, guaranteeing credit with traders, advising band members. By 1895, however, the Bureau of Indian Affairs dominated reservation life, deposing forceful Tag-Band chiefs, hiring irrigators, etc. Superintendents typically called Alchesay and other leaders into "council" simply to inform them of actions the Bureau intended to take, and to demand their cooperation in gaining Apache compliance. Despite such treatment, Alchesay patiently preached that young Apaches must learn to read and write English, learn skills to gain employment so as to compete with Anglo-Americans on their own terms. Even faced with serious generation gaps as an old man, Alchesay visited classrooms to urge students to stay in school, to take advantage of free instruction and books, free meals and clothing, to learn knowledge vitally needed to guarantee a White Mountain Apache future. Alchesay lived until 1928.

Chief Baha succeeded Alchesay as hereditary head chief, and carried on his foresightful admonishment. During the first decade of chieftainship, Baha's powers remained as limited as Alchesay's had been. In 1934, however, Congress enacted the Indian Reorganization Act which encouraged inhabitants of Indian reservations to establish reservation-wide democratic governments. After a great deal of discussion, the White Mountain Apaches on 15 August 1938 ratified a Tribal Constitution. It divided the reservation into electoral districts sending nine delegates to the tribal council. Canyon Day-Whiteriver-North Fork District elects three delegates. Three other districts elect two delegates each. A chairman and vice-chairman preside over the Council. Roe Clark served as first Chairman, succeeded by Purcell Kane and Fred Larzelere, beginning a succession of far-sighted leaders providing high quality guidance during a third of a century of self-government, particularly since the second World War.

84

CHIEF ALCHESAY AS AN OLD MAN.

In 1948, Lester Oliver began the first of what became several terms as tribal chairman, co-operating with Head Chief Baha. In 1950, Nelson Lupe, Sr., won election as chairman. An outstanding member of the first tribal council, he had been drafted by older chiefs and clan leaders to act as interpreter because of his command of English gained painfully at Sherman Institute and other boarding schools. During his first term, the Council made the Chairmanship a full-time, paid position. Talking with the Bureau of Indian Affairs Fire Control Officer for the reservation, Apache leaders including Lupe, Oliver and Chief Baha formed a concept of long-range development of the area's recreation income-producing potential. The Bureau had already shown the way partially toward such development. By World War II, Anglo-American anglers stormed Agency offices on fishing season opening day to purchase reservation fishing licenses, and the Agency built a fish hatchery on Diamond Creek to sustain yields of fish still taboo to the Apaches. Chief Baha urged resistant older people to open their reservation to tourists for a fee in spite of their well-founded distrust of Whites. Baha argued that White Mountain Apaches paid to stay in motels whenever they visited Holbrook or Globe. They purchased meals and even paid parking meters to park their automobiles. Before Baha died in 1953, he saw the Bureau official,

Silas O. Davis, retire in 1951 to go to work as Tribal Recreation Officer.

The Tribal Council laid the legal foundation for a semi-autonomous enterprise toward the end of Lupe's second term as chairman. In August, 1954, it enacted a resolution establishing the White Mountain Recreation Enterprise. The Council defined the general nature of the business as producing tribal income by selling hunting, fishing and camping permits, renting motel and hotel rooms, developing summer cabins and homes, tourist accommodations and camp grounds. During Lupe's administration the Council allowed liquor to be sold legally on Fort Apache Reservation.

Lester Oliver returned as Chairman in 1954 with Lupe as his Vice-Chairman. Davis and the Apache leaders planned to create an artificial reservoir in the Smith Park area of their reservation. The Salt River Valley Water Users' Association took legal action to prevent damming the stream. That Phoenix metropolitan area organization had long taken advantage of Arizona's water law doctrine of "prior appropriation" to claim or purchase rights to water in every watershed tributary to Salt River that it could, often hundreds of miles distant from Phoenix.

Reasoning that if anyone could claim water flowing on their reservation it was themselves, the White Mountain Apaches hired a contractor to carry out their plans. The Salt River Valley

Water Users' Association obtained a Maricopa County Superior Court injunction against construction. In a fine demonstration that they had not forgotten the tactics of their ancestors, the Apaches blocked all roads to the construction site with bulldozers and stationed guards armed with loaded rifles on the perimeter. Apache spokesmen informed state law enforcement officers that only tribal Indian police or U. S. marshalls could serve legal papers on the reservation.

Working around the clock, the construction crews completed the dam in twenty shifts in ten days. The Council named it in honor of Silas O. Davis, and named the resulting artificial reservoir Hawley Lake after their reservation superintendent. Legal arguments continued in U. S. District Court for another decade until a judge dismissed the action in 1966. During that decade, the White Mountain Apaches constructed no less than 26 additional recreational lakes. These bodies of water, plus game fish planting and other programs, laid foundations for profitable operation of reservation lands as a major Southwestern recreational resource.

Clinton Kessay won election as Tribal Chairman in that stressful year 1956, with Nelson Lupe as Vice-Chairman. The Tribe amended its constitution in 1958, lengthening the Chairman's term to four years, and providing for popular election of the two executives. Lester

HAWLEY LAKE, site of a major White Mountain Apache Enterprise recreation development with cabin sites overlooking the lakeshore.

Oliver won the first four-year term in 1958, to be re-elected in 1962. During the 1956-1959 period of Kessay's and Oliver's administrations, the tribal government carried out a Hawley Lake development plan. It built roads, laid water mains, installed power lines and constructed a public park. Moreover, it laid out 500 lots to lease for private cabin construction. As soon as Hawley Lake filled, Blue Lake National Fish Hatchery stocked it with 250,000 rainbow trout. The tribe set a policy of leasing half-acre or larger lots on or near the lake for $40 to $175 per year, according to proximity to lakeshore. Within three years after completion of basic installations, 450 of the lots had been leased, and 200 cabins finished or underway at costs ranging from $5,000 to $30,000. Cabins now number some 325.

The White Mountain Recreation Enterprise began to produce tribal income in 1958, and by 1962 employed 60 full-time Apache workers and 40 more seasonally. So successful was the plunge into recreational resource development that the Fort Apache Reservation program became a model for other Indian groups.

In 1966, Ron Lupe, Nelson's son, won election as Chairman. The following year, the Council split its commercial recreation program. A recreation service with a ranger force under a five-member board of directors administers hunting, fishing and camping. A White Mountain

90

Apache Enterprise governed by a separate five-member board appointed by the Council operates retail stores, trailer parks, restaurants, boat docks and similar commercial activities. In contrast to the Bureau of Indian Affairs, this tribal organization employs only six Anglo-Americans among some 100 full-time employees, and half as many part time workers. Both organizations directly and effectively attack the fundamental reservation problem of poverty stemming from historic isolation from the national economy. The White Mountain Apaches have found a peaceful three-forked path of profitable exploitation of the White man and his wants. In 1970, half a million visitors spent some $1,750,000 during a four-month period.

In 1970, Fred Banashley began a term as Chairman, carrying on the programs ably initiated by his predecessors. A high point in his young administration was federal approval of a large sum to finance further recreation facility development at Sunrise winter sports complex, destroyed by fire a year earlier. A 1,000 room lodge, 6,700 foot ski lift and cafe are under way.

Federal "Great Society" legislation provided the White Mountain Apaches with opportunities to earn money while carrying out useful social programs. Former Tribal Chairman Lester Oliver served as first Community Action Program Director. He initiated a Head Start pre-school

91

training program with ten instructors. A Neighborhood Youth Corps program employs needy youths who save summer earnings for the school year. A Mainstream program trains adults who find obtaining employment difficult because they lack skills.

Unlike almost all other reservation residents, the White Mountain Apaches maintain law and order with tribal funds. Captain Francis Dazen leads a force of nine officers and four matrons using radio-dispatched vehicles. They operate a modern jail in the Whiteriver municipal building. A judge and two associate justices hear cases in a Tribal Court established in 1940. Approximately half of the cases heard involve drunkenness or disorderly conduct.

CELEBRATION CALENDAR. The Fort Apache Reservation government began its labors without traditional Indian festivals to celebrate. Despite several decades living in the shadow of Spanish posts, the peaceful Apaches apparently never adopted even a Roman Catholic ceremonial calendar. The White Mountain Apaches have formulated new celebrations. The Fourth of July and Labor Day are the principal ones.

JULY FOURTH. Often White Mountain Apache families schedule girls' puberty ceremonies to coincide with the Fourth of July holiday. That event occasions a rodeo, often including a women's horserace, baseball games, *gahn* dances at night, as well as a gathering of Apaches to visit and talk to one another. The puberty ceremony performs much the same function for a girl that a "coming out party" does for the Anglo-American daughter of a socially prominent family, and more. The White Mountain Apache debut is an expensive affair. The family sponsoring such a ritual typically spends many months preparing for it. The initiate herself requires a brand new costume of highest quality, preferably buckskins. Ritual substances, including large quantities of pollen for blessing the initiate and those attending, must be gathered. Food must be stocked to feed several hundred spectators, since any Apache is welcome. Today only rich people on good terms with their kinsmen (whose labor they require) can give this *naihes* ceremony. The task of feeding the multitude becomes even more staggering when a family schedules a debut at Whiteriver on July Fourth. Families must obtain Tribal Council approval for the dates they pick.

Each initiate's family chooses a godmother to sponsor her, and accompany her throughout the four-day ritual. At one stage of the ceremony, this sponsor massages the initiate, who is stretched face-down over a pile of buckskins. Massaged correctly, she gains strength and endurance. An Apache religious singer conducts the ceremony, and traditionally the girls pays him a horse. Other men beat drums and sing both sacred songs accompanying the rite and

93

secular songs for dancing. Much drinking accompanies the "social dances" or *bigohjital,* often leading to fighting as well as courting.

The initiate goes through a long series of symbolic actions. In pursuit of fortune and health, she "walks in the footsteps of the gods" which are pollen-outlined foot prints on buckskins. Four times she runs around a feather tipped staff stuck into the ground, seeking long life, the most important goal of the ritual. Then she tossed four buckskins from her pile to the four cardinal directions to cast illness from her life. As the sun rises on the final morning, the singer paints white the face of the initiate kneeling on her buckskins, blesses her and her sponsor with pollen, rubs a symbol of the sun from his hand into her hair just when the sun strikes her. Tying a bit of shell to the initiate's forelock, the singer prays, and then extends to her two eagle feathers. She grasps them, and he leads her through the sacred bower of four white poles erected to symbolize the tent of the mythical White Painted Woman, followed by members of the audience.

FAIR AND RODEO. The White Mountain Apache celebrate Labor Day not as such, but as their occasion for an annual Tribal Fair and Rodeo. Decorated booths contain displays of garden crops, canned and baked goods, traditional Apache costumes and other arts and crafts products. Livestock appears in pens; and

94

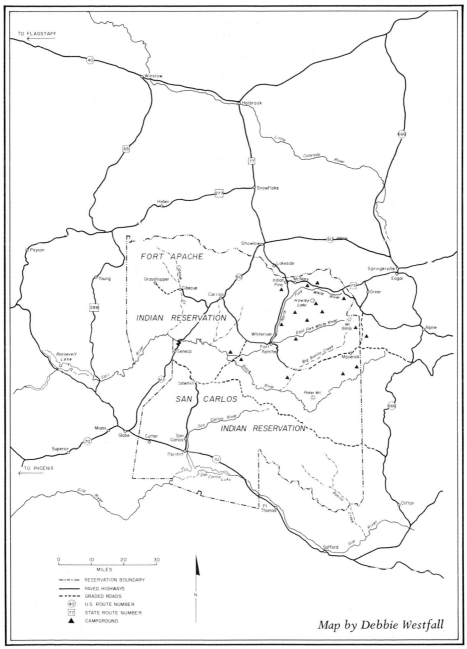

MAP 4. Recreation Resources of the Fort Apache Reservation, and principal travel routes.

the missions, schools and federal agencies set up exhibits. A contest in fried bread-making over an open fire provides daily interest. Events include not only the rodeo, but also baseball games and evening Indian dances.

THE FUTURE

The future stretches brightly before the White Mountain Apaches. Economically, they have made an increasingly successful transition to commercial cattle raising, sustained yield lumbering, and large-scale sale of recreational facilities. Not only have they found more ways of integrating their reservation economy into that of the nation than most Indians, but they have also generated excellent public relations with the dominant ethnic group while doing so.

Ethnic Survival

White Mountain Apaches can be expected to continue to increase rapidly in numbers and to maintain for the most part their Apachean genetic heritage. White Mountain bands forming the core of ancestors of the present reservation population apparently captured fewer slaves than other Western Apaches. Thus, they remain essentially Apachean. Yet they are not noticeably prejudiced against intermarriage with members of other ethnic groups. White Mountain Apache women who marry Anglo-Americans, Negroes and Chinese seem able to incorporate their children into reservation society.

CLAN SEGMENTATION. The first people to hear when a drinking party begins are clansmen, and they expect the most generous portions when they arrive. Not only alcoholic beverages, but also pickup trucks, saddles and rifles are regularly loaned among fellow clan members. Yet a century of reservation life has altered clan behavior, and seems clearly destined to generate still more "branching." People refer to local members of a clan as a "branch." These local branches have acquired an importance on the reservation they did not possess when Western Apaches ranged freely and occupied dispersed small settlements. Informal leadership by local clan elders has emerged. At the same time, prohibitions on marriage between members of related clans have weakened. Local clan branches may be expected to continue to gain social strength at the expense of the traditional ideal of the clan integrated across space. Economic imperatives in contemporary village and town settlement almost guarantee continuation of the trend toward increased importance to the White Mountain Apache individual of clan members living nearby, and lessened awareness of distant clan members. Residents of modern settlements naturally tend to know one another better than outsiders, to speak a distinct dialect, and to develop patterns of mutual trust and cooperation. They therefore tend to marry one another, placing a strain on prohibitions against marriage within related clans.

ALCOHOLISM AND DRINKING. There are some dark clouds on the White Mountain Apache horizon. One is high incidence of drinking with consequent brawls, accidents, homicides and suicides. The consequences of the Spanish colonial policy of debauching conquered Apaches after 1786 persist. Those consequences will continue into the foreseeable future.

The most important contribution Spaniards made to White Mountain Apache drinking technology proved to be knowledge of how to brew maize beer. This actually provides valuable nutrients and undoubtedly helps to vary a monotonous diet. While Agent John P. Clum could close the liquor section of the San Carlos post trader's store, he could not terminate home brew production. Alcohol provided some temporary relief, at least, from psychological and physical stresses of internment. The millenarian movements of Nakaidkolinni, Daslahdn and Silas John Edwards attest to the continued stress under which White Mountain Apaches labor. People struggled simply to survive, yet men typically had time to spend because they remained underemployed. Drinking and gambling offered some release.

By the time economic development began, a pattern of pathological drinking was firmly established. Even with economic expansion

98

came a copious flow of bootlegged intoxicants as well as hard-drinking examples at McNary, with its hundreds of underpaid workers.

All the economic achievements of tribal government have not ended psychological stress on individuals. Experience here and elsewhere shows that many Indians find the decision-making required by autonomous self-government and economic integration produces greater anxiety than taking orders from an authoritarian superintendent or similar authority figure. Multiplication of decisions to be made surely must be anticipated as White Mountain Apache economic enterprises expand. Thus, one can but anticipate continuation of drinking as a serious social problem for the White Mountain Apaches. Community Health Representatives may help individual drinkers, but seem unlikely to solve the problems of all. The Christian missions have preached on the subject for decades without achieving the millenium.

NATIVE CURING. White Mountain Apaches readily consult Anglo-American physicians. Yet they also believe scientific medicine to be defective in diagnosis of causes of disease and provision for supernatural protection against it. So strong is Apache belief in native diagnosis and ritual protection today, as the confusion among Christians becomes starkly clear, that native medical practice may be expected to flourish for many years.

PENTECOSTALISM. Continued White Mountain Apache concern for individual well-being and the nature of Pentecostal Christian mission preaching will similarly favor the growth of Pentecostal congregations on Fort Apache Reservation in the immediate future. At the same time, as other denominations stress development of Apache congregational self-reliance, Apache Christians can be expected to develop denomination allegiances that become seriously competitive with other social ties. Probably denominational membership will segregate along socio-economic status lines.

WELFARE AND AGING. Since White Mountain Apaches believe older persons are particularly suited to act as witches, fear of witchcraft motivates attention to the needs of the aging. As Christian missionaries succeed in converting Apaches to their beliefs and fear of witchcraft declines, the gap between generations widens. Although the wild plant food utilization program begun in 1971 gives older Apaches a respected teacher's role, older residents of the Fort Apache Reservation face the same uncertain future as Anglo-Americans of comparable age.

HOUSING. Enthusiastic White Mountain Apache participation in the mutual help housing program indicates future residence in homes of Anglo-American style. Conversion to Christianity has diminished fear of the dead that led to burning huts in which a person died. Social pressure from boarding school and college students who want to invite friends home, but are embarrassed to bring them to a plank shack or brush-covered hut, provides strong motivation for improving homes. Eventually, White Mountain Apaches may be expected to reside in homes not very different from those off reservation, even to landscape plantings such as those already underway at mutual help project homes. The main difference will be Apache utilization of lumber from the tribal sawmills.

DEMOCRATIC GOVERNMENT. Perhaps the very quality and strength of White Mountain Apache leadership and its outstanding achievements have kept it relatively elite. Much of the population seems unaware of Tribal Council actions, and most people prefer to settle disputes without recourse to tribal police or court. The wider Apache participation in tribal government becomes, the more democratic will it be. Yet, the college students working summers in tribal offices appear to constitute the main source of new recruits, and they themselves comprise a new type of educated elite. Democratization appears uncertain.

SUGGESTED READING

THESE BOOKS CONTAIN firsthand accounts of the White Mountain Apaches at different times in their history, and should be available in major libraries. Shorter and more technical reports may be found in several scientific journals.

This list is short because published discussions of Western Apaches are largely of low quality, although voluminous, and seldom specifically deal with the White Mountain Apache people.

BALDWIN, GORDON C. *The Warrior Apaches.* Tucson: Dale Stuart King, 1965.

The best popular account of Western Apaches, easily read and copiously illustrated.

BASSO, KEITH H. *The Gift of Changing Woman.* Anthropological Paper N° 76, Bureau of American Ethnology Bulletin 196, 1966.

Fullest scientific description and analysis of the White Mountain Apache girls' puberty rite.

Western Apache Witchcraft. Tucson: University of Arizona Anthropological Paper N° 15, 1969.

Describing White Mountain Apache witchcraft beliefs, this scientific analysis contributes to general theory about witchcraft.

DOBYNS, HENRY F. *Lance, Ho! Containment of the Western Apaches by the Royal Spanish Garrison at Tucson.* Lima: Editorial Estudios Andinos, 1964.

One chapter of this pamphlet translates Spanish reports of the 1782 May Day assault on the post.

GODDARD, PLINY E. *Myths and Tales from the White Mountain Apache.* Anthropological Publications of the American Museum of Natural History, No. 24, Part 2.

GOODWIN, GRENVILLE *Myths and Tales of the White Mountain Apache.* Memoir N° 39, American Folklore Society, 1939.

The Social Organization of the Western Apache. Chicago: University of Chicago Press, 1942.

A great ethnographic report, this work is crammed with cultural and historical data. Basic reference.

MOOREHEAD, MAX L. *The Apache Frontier: Jacobo Ugarte and Spanish-Indian Relations in Northern New Spain, 1767-1791.* Norman: University of Oklahoma Press, 1968.

Although focused on one official, this history provides more data on Western Apaches in Spanish times than any other.

OGLE, RALPH H. *Federal Control of the Western Apaches, 1848-1886.* Historical Society of New Mexico, 1940. (1970 reprint)

A still sound historical summary.

SPICER, EDWARD H. *Cycles of Conquest.* Tucson: University of Arizona Press, 1962.

Apache discussions contain the best synthesis of Western Apache ethnic history in print. Technical but readable.

THRAPP, DAN L. *The Conquest of Apacheria.* Norman: University of Oklahoma Press, 1967.

An excellent historical summary with some errors on details supplements and expands Ogle.

WHARFIELD, H. B. *With Scouts and Cavalry at Fort Apache.* Tucson: Arizona Pioneers' Historical Society, 1965.

Not very profound, this partial autobiography evokes the twilight years of Fort Apache.

THE AUTHOR

HENRY F. DOBYNS, Professor of Anthropology
at Prescott College, is a former professor and
chairman of the Department of Anthropology at
the University of Kentucky. Earlier he served as
Lecturer and Senior Research Associate in the
Department of Anthropology at Cornell Univer-
sity. There he coordinated the Comparative
Studies of Cultural Change and Andean Indian
Community Research-and-Development
(Ecuador, Peru, Bolivia) programs. A native of
Arizona, Dobyns earned the B. A. and M. A.
degrees from the University of Arizona, and the
Ph.D. degree from Cornell University. He con-
ducted anthropological research for the
Hualapai, Havasupai, Papago, and Pima tribes of
Arizona.

Dobyns collaborated with Dr. Robert C. Euler
in writing two earlier Indian Tribal Series vol-
umes, *The Havasupai People,* and *The Hopi
People.* He has published two books on Peruvian
Indian communities, *The Social Matrix of Peru-
vian Indigenous Communities* in English, and
Comunidades Campesinas del Peru in Spanish.
With Dr. Mario C. Vázquez, Dobyns edited
Migración e Integración en el Perú on Peruvian
internal migration. For the Arizona Pioneers'
Historical Society, he edited *Hepah, California!
The Journal of Cave Johnson Couts from
Monterey, Nuevo Leon, Mexico, to Los Angeles,
California, during the years 1848-1849.*

106